British
Columbia's

Best
Camping
Adventures

*Southwestern BC
and Vancouver Island*

Jayne Seagrave

HERITAGE HOUSE

CANADIAN CATALOGUING IN PUBLICATION DATA

Seagrave, Jayne 1961-
British Columbia's Best Camping Adventures

ISBN 1-895811-55-4

1. Camp sites, facilities, etc.—British Columbia—Guidebooks
2. Outdoor recreation—British Columbia—Guidebooks
3. British Columbia—Guidebooks
I. Title.
FC3807.S45 1998   917.1104'4   C98-910125-8

First Edition 1998

Heritage House wishes to acknowledge the support of Department of Canadian Heritage through the Book Publishing Industry Development Program, the Canada Council, and Cultural Services Branch of the Government of British Columbia for supporting various aspects of its publishing program.

Front Cover Photo: Saltery Bay Provincial Park
                     Strathcona Provincial Park
Back Cover Photos: Inland Lake
                     Saltery Bay
Cover, book design, and typesetting: Darlene Nickull
Photos: Andrew Dewberry
Edited by: Audrey McClellan

HERITAGE HOUSE PUBLISHING COMPANY LTD.
Unit #8 - 17921 55th Ave., Surrey, BC V3S 6C4

Printed in Canada

ACKNOWLEDGEMENTS

While my name is the one associated with this book, a number of people have nurtured my enthusiasm and facilitated the book's completion.

The people at BC Parks have been superb, granting me their time and the latest information on park amenities. I am specifically indebted to Cheryl Noble and Don Maculay for assisting me and giving permission to reproduce some of their photographs. I am also grateful to numerous park administrators who answered questions and gave me their opinions and observations.

The staff at Heritage House has again been very supportive of my desire to write a book on the best campgrounds. Darlene, Rodger, Pat, John, and Diane all educated me about the multifaceted publishing process and have given me valuable help and guidance to bring this work to completion, while Audrey McClellan did a superb job in editing the initial manuscript.

Friends and family assisted with site visits and the necessary research of checking out campground access roads, interpretative programs, thunderboxes, adventure playgrounds, hiking trails, and showers. Elizabeth Seagrave, Sally Leivers, and Susan Leivers all took an active role in this research.

Finally, my camping and life partner Andrew Dewberry watched and did not complain as our hobby developed and I requested numerous weekends away from home to collect data for this book. His patience, support, and affection for me and for my aspirations are my greatest inspiration.

FOREWORD

Some people live to ski. They get excited when the first snows of winter herald the onset of the ski season and they can't wait to "hit the slopes." Others appreciate the fall, when the fish are running and they can spend hours on or by the water, testing their skill with a fly rod. Mountain bikers are excited by spring when they are granted access to the higher elevation trails.

I love spring because it is the beginning of the camping season. Like many others in British Columbia, I live to camp and find it difficult to comprehend how others might not share my enthusiasm. Hopefully this book will persuade the reluctant to take the plunge and give camping a try.

After my first book, *Provincial and National Park Campgrounds in British Columbia: A Complete Guide*, was published in 1997, I took part in a number of book signings, radio phone-in programs, and newspaper interviews about camping in B.C. During the course of these events I spoke to numerous campers and realised my love for camping and for the excellent facilities offered in B.C. was shared by thousands of others, many with considerably more years of experience than I had. We all shared the same ingrained passion and unadulterated enthusiasm for the pursuit of the perfect camping experience.

Provincial and National Park Campgrounds in B.C. provides good summary information on over 160 provincial and national parks across B.C., and it stimulated many campers to leave their favourite park. I was surprised at the number of people I spoke to who always camped in the same location, returning year after year to the campground they knew well. I also spoke to many people in the southwest quadrant of B.C. who requested more detailed information about campgrounds closer to home. Often these individuals had young children or other considerations and were not prepared to drive hundreds of miles to a campground in the Rockies or Kootenays, no matter how idyllic it sounded.

British Columbia's Best Camping Adventures: Southwestern B.C. And Vancouver Island has been written for these people, to encourage exploration of almost 40 provincial, national, and forestry service campgrounds in the most populated area of the province. It is designed for veteran campers and novices, for those who camp in recreational vehicles (RVs) or tents and who wish information not only on the campground itself, but also on its history, development, and the recreational opportunities provided both within and adjacent to its boundaries.

Camping is a wonderful, fun, relaxing activity. It is also a fantastic way to experience the beauty of B.C. At relatively little cost. The aim of this book is to encourage more people to do just that: to undertake a camping adventure in southwestern B.C. And to share my passion.

CONTENTS

INTRODUCTION

British Columbia's provincial park system makes an annual contribution of over $420 million to the provincial economy. For every dollar government spends on park operations, visitors spend nine dollars, with more than one third of visitors' expenditures coming from out-of-province residents. Parks generate $170 million in tax revenue for the provincial and national governments and support over 9500 direct and indirect jobs.

This information is from a 1995 report that Coopers & Lybrand Management Consultants produced for B.C.'s Ministry of Environment, Lands and Parks. The Coopers & Lybrand study estimated that, based on forecasted growth and development, B.C.'s parks could account for well over $600 million of provincial gross domestic revenues by 2002.

These figures illustrate the success of B.C.'s parks and are testimony to the valued service they provide both residents and tourists. In 1996, 2.7 million people visited B.C. campgrounds, an increase of 12 percent over the previous five years. Predictions about the future of camping in provincial, national, and forestry service campgrounds are good. The provincial parks branch is taking over more of the BC Forestry Service (BCFS) wilderness sites and equipping them with superior camping facilities (fresh water, wood, pit toilets, fire pits, and picnic tables). This development, coupled with the public's increasing love of camping, ensures this is not a recreational pursuit subject to the whims of fashion. Camping is here to stay!

Camping Myths

One of the most common urban legends tells of the Vancouver family that decided to go camping the second week in August. They telephoned the Discover Camping Reservation Service to be told that all reservable spaces in all campgrounds were fully booked for the rest of the month; no space at Rathtrevor, Miracle Beach, Golden Ears, Porteau Cove, Manning, or anywhere else. So they stayed at home, cursing the influx of tourists and reminiscing of times gone by when there was always accommodation. This family, frequently cited by some as their reason not to camp, was unaware that with a little foresight and preparation a successful camping adventure could have been theirs.

While BC Parks facilities are undoubtedly becoming more popular, it is possible to find room in some fantastic locations. If you leave home at 5:00 p.m. on Friday of the Labour Day long weekend, you will probably not find a space. But if you arrive at a number of the campgrounds detailed in this book around midday on a Friday, even on holiday weekends, you will probably secure a spot. Although the key to staying in some of the most popular provincial park campgrounds is to make a reservation, the secret to finding space in others is forward planning to ensure arrival before the busy Friday evening period or to stay during the week. Alternatively, you might plan to camp in May, early June, or September. If you can select these months, you will be blessed with some of the quietest camping experiences. With a little bit of preparation, there is no excuse not to take full advantage of the camping potential in beautiful southwestern B.C.

What to Expect at a Provincial, National, or British Columbia Forest Service Campground

Watch for a provincial campground roadsign.

National and provincial park campgrounds are well signposted on major highways. A sign two kilometres before the campground turnoff is the first warning campers receive, followed by another sign 400 metres from the campground. The second sign gives directions to the access road. If a campground is full or closed, the park operator will post notices on these roadside signs stating this fact.

In contrast, there is little or no roadside notification of most BCFS sites, and you may need to locate them on a map or by following instructions in books such as this. BCFS sites are indicated in the *BC Recreational Atlas* (available at bookstores and at BC Ferries gift shops) and on maps produced by the Ministry of Forests. You can obtain these maps by calling the Vancouver Forest Region Office at (250) 751-7001. (This office covers Vancouver Island and the Lower Mainland.) These sites are often located off logging roads, which can be extremely rough in places. Consequently, reaching these wilderness campgrounds is an adventure and not recommended for those concerned about their vehicle's suspension. If you have a truck or 4x4 you shouldn't have a problem, and some BCFS campgrounds (including a number of those detailed in this book) do not necessitate such a drive. BCFS campgrounds tend to be smaller and less organised than those in provincial and national parks. It is often impossible to see where one spot ends and another starts. Chapter 7 includes more general information on BCFS sites.

If you have a reservation at a provincial campground (see below), your reserved site will be listed at the park entrance. For those without a reservation, the biggest thrill upon arrival at a campground is deciding which spot to settle in. Depending on the season, time of day, and location of the park, this decision may have already been made for you, as the park could be full or have only a couple of places left. Some parks have areas specifically designated for tents, while most provincial and national parks have spots suitable for either RVs or tenters. A number of parks offer "double spots," ideal for two families camping together, and pull-through spots for the larger RVs. There is usually a map of the campground at the entrance, which details where these spots are to be found.

Once you have established which sites are restricted you will need to "cruise" the campground so you can pick a spot. This is known as the "campground waltz" and it involves numerous trips in both forward and reverse gear around the campground as you attempt to find the perfect space. If you drive a large RV, you will also do the campground shuffle. This jig requires all but one member of the camping party to leave the vehicle and position themselves around its perimeter. The remaining party member, usually a male, is left in the driver's seat to delicately shuffle the vehicle forwards and backwards as other team members raise and lower their hands, exchange positions, shout directions and encouragement, and slap the side of the RV until it comes to rest in the correct position. This is entertaining for observers, especially when some of the larger RVs attempt to dance.

Reservations

Campers with reservations:

- Check the campsite allocation list for your name, campsite number.

- Occupy the campsite you have been assigned.

1-800-689-9025
DISCOVER CAMPING

Drop-in Campers

Campers without reservations:

- Occupy a site NOT marked RESERVED.

- An attendant will come by to register you.

- To reserve a site, call the phone number below.

1-800-689-9025
DISCOVER CAMPING

Information boards include maps and campground information.

Campsites by a beach, lake, river, or creek are most desirable, so head for these first. Avoid areas of stagnant water (mosquito breeding grounds) or spots close to the "thunderboxes" (pit toilets), which may exude unpleasant odours (especially during the warm summer months), attract flies, and disturb you with banging doors. At first glance, spots near the flush toilets and showers may seem convenient, especially if you have young children, but remember that between 5:00 p.m. And 11:00 p.m. And again from 7:00 a.m. to 11:00 a.m., most people at the campground will be visiting these facilities and walking past your site in order to do it.

As you drive around the campground, make a mental note of your preferences and then claim your most desirable spot by parking a vehicle there. Alternatively, leave some item, such as a water jug or a plastic table cloth, on the picnic table to state to the world that this spot is taken.

When you are established in your new home, you are ready to explore the campground. Your first stop should be a return to the information board at the campground entrance, as this will have a full map of the campground, details of any hazards in the area, lists of interpretative programs available, information about other campgrounds in the region, leaflets, and maps. A number of the larger provincial parks have camp hosts. These are often retired couples who volunteer to live in the campground for at least one month and offer advice and assistance to visitors. They supply maps, park guides, and handouts, and are an excellent source of information about the area. Camp hosts will have a little sign by their site that tells visitors whether they are on or off duty, so campers know when they can disturb them. Often the hosts walk around and visit campers, checking to see if anything is needed.

You will want to familiarize yourself with the facilities available at the campground. All provincial and national park campgrounds included in this book have the basics: water, wood, pit toilets, picnic tables, and fire pits. Larger campgrounds might have sani-stations, flush toilets, showers, wheelchair access, interpretative and Jerry Rangers programs (see below), visitors centres, and group camping. Washroom facilities are generally well maintained and clean, and unlike many BCFS campgrounds, never run out of toilet tissue. Gravel camping spots are tidied and raked after each visitor departs, garbage is regularly collected, and there are bins for recycling. In contrast, the facilities at BCFS sites vary considerably. It is rare to find a picnic table per site, few have toilets segregated along gender lines or with toilet doors which stretch to the floor (and remember to take your own toilet paper if you plan to stay at one of these sites), and fresh water has to be collected from nearby streams and rivers. What these campgrounds lack in basic comforts, however, they generally make up for by granting access to some of the most remote areas of the province.

A park attendant collects fees (cash only) during the early evening hours. As you might expect, camping fees vary depending on the facilities provided; campgrounds with showers tend to be the most expensive, while less developed campgrounds have lower fees. No fees are charged for BCFS sites. At the time of writing, fees ranged from $6.00 to $15.50 for provincial parks and up to $22.00 for national parks (GST included). In national parks you also are requested to pay for firewood. You can stay for as many nights as you want up to a maximum of 14 nights in both provincial and national parks. The attendant will post a receipt at your spot that displays the date you intend to leave.

Park attendants, like this one at Saltery Bay, will come around to collect fees during the early evening hours.

Although some campgrounds are open throughout the year, fees for individual camping spots are only collected from April to October. Residents of B.C. who are 65 or older may camp for half price in provincial parks between Labour Day and June 14. From June 15 to Labour Day, full rates apply. Individuals with disabilities camp for free if they have a BC Parks Disabled Access Pass.

The park attendants who collect fees are good sources of information on weather conditions, local activities, the best fishing locations, etc. They also tend to be interesting characters, attributable perhaps to the long periods of time they have been working outdoors, operating what one described to me as "a huge open-air hotel."

Interpretative Programs

Interpretative programs take the form of talks, presentations, slide shows, walks, or field trips. BC Parks staff members or guest speakers present informative instruction on any number of topics, from the local fauna and flora or local history to the night sky. Most presentations take place in the early evening, often in a specially designed amphitheatre, a feature of most of the larger parks. The events last about an hour and are generally designed to appeal to every age group.

The knowledge and enthusiasm of BC Parks staff are frequently supplemented by some of the colourful campers who provide unscripted personal anecdotes, observations, questions, and comments that add to the enjoyment of the evening.

The programs are casual affairs. Remember to take along bug repellent and a blanket, as sitting on a cold log bench for an hour as the sun goes down can become a chilling experience.

Jerry Rangers Programs

In 1984, BC Parks started Jerry Rangers, a program aimed at creating in children "an understanding of conservation issues and knowledge of the natural and cultural environment as they relate to the provincial park system." This program is offered at the larger parks. Check at the visitors centre or on the park notice board for details.

A child joins by obtaining a Jerry Rangers Certificate from a BC Parks staff member at the park he or she is visiting and by promising to take care of the park by following a number of rules outlined on the back of the certificate. Jerry Rangers participants take part in games, crafts, and other activities. The programs are geared to the environment of each individual park and have names such as "Slippery Slimy Slugs," "The Bear Facts," and "Just Squidding Around." Children can earn Jerry Rangers stickers by taking part in activities. For example, they receive the Nature Nut sticker for learning about a park's natural history, the Dogged Detective sticker for developing investigative skills to unravel park mysteries, the Safety Sense sticker for learning hiking, boating, and swimming safety skills, and the Earth Explorer sticker for developing orienteering and survival skills. During the summer months, these activities occur twice daily in the larger parks and are a great way for kids to make friends in a fun, educational environment. BC Parks requires that an adult accompany children taking part in these programs.

Reservations

One of the biggest camping success stories is the reservation system, introduced in 1996 by BC Parks. It allows campers to reserve spots at 45 of the more popular provincial and national parks in B.C. During its first hugely successful year of operation, the service received 88,000 phone calls and 40,500 reservations were made. It is now established as a permanent fixture.

The advantage of reservations is that they assure accommodation for the night. For those with children or with commitments that prevent an early getaway for a camping weekend, the reservation system does away with uncertainty and ensures the joy of camping is not denied. However, unlike the system operating in Washington state, where clients select their own spot, the B.C. service gives campers no say over the spot designated to them. You could find yourself located next to a well-used thunderbox, at the busy entrance to the campground, or at a particularly small site.

To make a reservation, phone Discover Camping Campground Reservation Service at 1-800-689-9025 between 7:00 a.m. And 7:00 p.m. (Pacific Time) Monday to Friday and between 9:00 a.m. And 5:00 p.m. on Saturday and Sunday. This service is available from March 1 to September 15. At the time of writing the fee to reserve was $6.00 per night to a

Southwestern B.C. Campgrounds Accepting Reservations

1.	Alice Lake	28.	Montague Harbour
2.	Bamberton*	45.	Pacific Rim
10.	Cultus Lake	34.	Porpoise Bay
12.	Englishman River Falls*	35.	Porteau Cove
14.	French Beach	36.	Prior Centennial
15.	Golden Ears	37.	Rathtrevor
16.	Goldstream*	38.	Rolley Lake
17.	Gordon Bay	39.	Saltery Bay
25.	Manning	40.	Sasquatch
26.	Miracle Beach		

Numbers denote the Discover Camping Reference Number.
* Campground not detailed in this book.

Camping spot at Rathtrevor Provincial Campsite.

maximum of $18.00 for 3 to 14 nights. This fee is subject to GST. Campers pay the reservation and campsite fees by Mastercard or Visa when making the reservation. You can reserve a site up to three months in advance, but a reservation must be made at least two days prior to your arrival at the campsite. You can cancel a reservation via voice mail 24 hours a day.

Prospective campers can check the availability of campsites at campgrounds that accept reservations by using a touch-tone phone. Enter the campground's reference number (see the list in the box) and the dates you would like to stay. If a space is available, you can book it by speaking to a Discover Camping representative.

If you do not have a reservation, campsites are available on a first come, first served basis. When you arrive at a campground, a notice board at the gate will provide details on which spots are reserved. Only a percentage of campsites in each campground are reservable, although this can be as high as 75 percent. (If a campground profiled in this book accepts reservations, I will indicate this in the "Facilities" section.)

Defining "The Best"

In writing a book on the best camping venues, I know I'm bound to be criticised for the choices I make. What appeals to one camper may disappoint another. Retired people seek different activities than large families or young couples, and while one person may think the sound of the adjacent babbling brook will be conducive to a good night's sleep, another will curse this intrusion that invades slumber and demands nightly excursions to the nearest washroom.

The campgrounds in this text have been selected to appeal to a broad audience. With the exception of four locations in the chapter on BCFS free campgrounds, they are limited to provincial (and one national) sites. Although there are many superb private camping facilities in the province, these are not reviewed. The campgrounds selected are located on Vancouver Island south of Campbell River, on the Sunshine Coast, and on the mainland west of Princeton and south of Lillooet. Many are located in areas of outstanding natural beauty with a diverse range of recreational pursuits.

I primarily chose places where holidaymakers can easily spend a week, not only enjoying the campground itself, but also the surrounding environment. For the most part the selected campgrounds are suitable for both RVs and tents, and over half of the 30 national and provincial campgrounds listed in the book accept reservations.

How to Use This Book

In an attempt to cover a broad range of camping preferences, I have included government-run campgrounds with the most comprehensive provisions alongside those with the most basic. BC Parks statistics suggest that many campers, especially those with young families, appreciate the facilities offered by the larger campgrounds located close to centres of population, so these make up the majority of entries in this book. In addition to providing such camping luxuries as flush toilets and showers, these large campgrounds often have interpretative talks and Jerry Rangers programs (see above).

At the other end of the scale, the facilities at the free BCFS sites are rudimentary (for example, these campgrounds tend to be small, often with fewer than 10 campsites, only one pit toilet, two picnic tables, and no tap water or wood). What these campgrounds lack in organization, they make up for with their wonderful wilderness locations.

The book is divided into seven chapters. Each chapter focuses on the best campgrounds in a particular category—the best campgrounds for families, for hiking, with beaches, on islands, and for kissing, as well as marine and BCFS campgrounds. At the end of each chapter I have recommended other campgrounds that may also be regarded as "the best" in these categories. In the appendix I suggest additional reading and provide

Firewood and water is supplied at most campgrounds.

addresses where you can obtain more information to supplement your enjoyment of B.C.

Each campground entry contains a number of subheadings. After the introduction, which justifies why the campground is included as one of the best in the category, "History" gives a synopsis of the area's past. "Location" tells how to find the campground and describes its geographical features. "Facilities" lists the number of camping spots and the services (i.e., showers, toilets, wood, water, reservations, etc.). "Recreational Activities" outlines what opportunities, if any, the campground offers for hiking, boating, cycling, fishing, wildlife observation, and family activities, as well as activities that are available in the surrounding area. Finally, "Summary" gives some personal or anecdotal information about the campground. Numerous photographs have also been included and maps on page 20 and 21 show the location of each campground.

Camping Tips

One of the joys of camping is learning the little tricks that make it easier. Here are a few tips:

1. If the campground does not have a shower, leave a full plastic water container in the sun all day long and wash in warm water in the evening.
2. Take a water container and a funnel to collect water from the pump.
3. Carry a small amount of dry wood to make it easy to start a fire.
4. Cook vegetables (e.g. mushrooms, tomatoes, zucchini, peppers, and onions) by wrapping them in aluminium foil, sealing them in with spices.
5. If you do not have a reservation, try to arrive at a campground before 5:00 p.m., as the most popular hours for arrival are between 5:00 p.m. And 8:00 p.m.
6. It's a good idea to keep a keyring-size flashlight in your pocket for emergencies and for nightly excursions to the washroom.
7. Axes, matches, dry paper, plastic bags, rope, flashlights, candles, and aluminium foil are all camping basics. Add toilet paper to that list if you are camping in BCFS sites.
8. Spread a tarp under the tent for extra protection against the damp.
9. Keep one set of clothes specifically for wearing by the campfire so you have only one outfit smelling of woodsmoke.
10. Dry wet wood by propping logs against the fire pit.

Now you are ready for a camping adventure...GO FOR IT!

Camping Etiquette

There are a number of unwritten camping rules. For the most part they are common sense, and they exist to ensure all campers have a good time.

1. Quiet time is from 11:00 p.m. to 7:00 a.m. Provincial and national parks close their gates during this time to prevent arrivals from disturbing the peace.

2. In late summer and on island campgrounds, the threat of forest fires may result in a ban on campfires. Check park information boards to determine status. At all times, light fires only in metal fire pits.

3. Store food in your vehicle or in airtight containers. With over 100,000 black bears in B.C., this is not a rule to ignore. If you do not have a vehicle and are in an area frequented by bears, hang food in bags suspended well out on a tree branch, at least four metres above the ground.

4. To protect vegetation, camp only in the designated areas.

5. Reduce waste and recycle as much as possible. BC Parks provides dispensers for recycling, while in some BCFS campgrounds campers are requested to pack out what they pack in.

6. Each year, campers in B.C. parks burn the equivalent of 2000 logging trucks of wood. One of the many advantages B.C.'s provincial parks have over national parks, private campgrounds, and United States campgrounds is that firewood is provided at no charge (although this may change in the future). Wood should not be wasted; take only as much as you need.

7. In government parks, checkout time is midday and the maximum length of stay is 14 days per year in any one park. There are no limits to the length of time campers can stay at a BCFS site. A camping party is regarded as a family from the same address or a maximum of four people 13 years or older, of which one must be over the age of 16.

8. Cutting branches and picking flowers, berries, or mushrooms is prohibited in provincial and national parks.

9. Clean your campsite on departure, making sure all food remains and garbage have been cleared away. This is particularly important in the BCFS sites where there are no attendants.

10. Pets should be kept on a leash in all areas of the campground.

11. Do not use your fire pit as a garbage disposal. Partly burnt food tempts wildlife, and blackened cans are an annoyance to whoever follows.

12. Only one camping vehicle is allowed per campsite. This vehicle must fit comfortably without damaging the location or causing a nuisance to other campers. The only exceptions are when an additional vehicle is being towed or when group members arrive from a common home address in separate vehicles (the commuter vehicle must be registered at the same address as the registered party).

13. Do not take powerboats near swimmers. Try to avoid disturbing the tranquillity of those enjoying the beach by revving engines excessively.

14. Alcohol is not permitted in the public areas of BC Parks but *is* allowed on your camping spot.

Maps

Maps on these next two pages are provided as a guide only. Use BC Parks maps referenced in the appendix for more accurate locations. The black circled numbers are highway references. The white circled numbers indicate campgrounds covered in this book. The number preceding the campground name in the key is the campground's reference number in the text. The number in brackets gives the page reference.

Vancouver Island

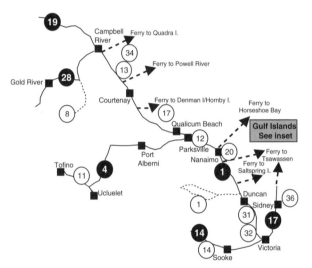

Campground #, Campground name, Page reference

- 31. Bamberton (41)
- 35. Beaumont Marine (117)
- 17. Fillongley (92)
- 14. French Beach (79)
- 32. Goldstream (41)
- 1. Gordon Bay (23)
- 13. Miracle Beach (76)
- 15. Montague Harbour (84)
- 20. Newcastle Island Marine (106)
- 11. Pacific Rim National (68)
- 36. Portland Island (117)
- 18. Prior Centennial (96)
- 12. Rathtrevor Beach (71)
- 16. Ruckle (88)
- 21. Sidney Spit Marine (111)
- 34. Smelt Bay (99)
- 8. Strathcona (52)

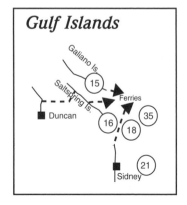

Gulf Islands

Vancouver Coast, Mountains

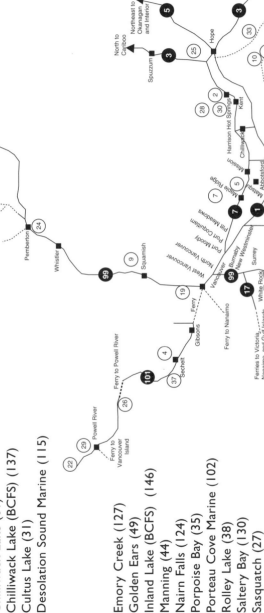

Campground #, Campground name, Page reference

9. Alice Lake (57)
23. Birkenhead Lake (120)
28. Chehalis Lake (BCFS) (142)
10. Chilliwack Lake (61)
27. Chilliwack Lake (BCFS) (137)
3. Cultus Lake (31)
22. Desolation Sound Marine (115)

25. Emory Creek (127)
7. Golden Ears (49)
29. Inland Lake (BCFS) (146)
6. Manning (44)
24. Nairn Falls (124)
4. Porpoise Bay (35)
19. Porteau Cove Marine (102)
5. Rolley Lake (38)
26. Saltery Bay (130)
2. Sasquatch (27)
33. Skagit Valley (65)
37. Smuggler Cove Marine (117)
30. Weaver Lake (BCFS) (150)

THE BEST FAMILY CAMPGROUNDS

Gordon Bay • Sasquatch • Cultus Lake
Porpoise Bay • Rolley Lake

In choosing the best family campgrounds, I have attempted to offer variety, while at the same time selecting larger campgrounds which have the best facilities in B.C.'s parks (i.e., all have showers and flush toilets).

Gordon Bay on Vancouver Island has a sandy lakeside beach, excellent facilities, and is located in one of the warmest areas in the province. **Sasquatch**, on the mainland, also has wonderful beaches and gives you the choice of three different camping locations and four lakes of varying size. The third campground, **Cultus Lake**, offers a number of family-based activities. The fourth recommendation is **Porpoise Bay** on the Sunshine Coast, which has a beautiful beach and water-centred activities close to a major centre of population. Finally, I chose **Rolley Lake** because even though it is smaller and quieter than the other options, it still has all facilities.

All these campgrounds provide interpretative programs and Jerry Rangers programs during the peak summer months.

1. Gordon Bay Provincial Park

McDonald, French Beach, Bamberton, Goldstream, and Gordon Bay are all beautiful campgrounds near the main population centre of southern Vancouver Island and in close proximity to each other, which makes choosing one to stay at a difficult decision. Gordon Bay must be regarded as the best family campground, as it offers something for every age group, has excellent facilities, is only a short distance from a picturesque community, and yet is remote enough to have that "get away from it all" feel. There can be no better place for sun lovers, as Gordon Bay Provincial Park's 49 hectares are located in one of the warmest valleys on Vancouver Island. The mountains pressing close around Cowichan Lake produce a heat trap that ensures the highest average daily temperature in Canada. In the summer this means 24 degrees Celsius. The waters of Lake Cowichan supply relief from this heat, as do the shady camping spots.

History

The area has a rich logging history that still lives on today, as you can see on the mountain slopes that surround the valley. Logging started here in the 1880s, when oxen were used to haul felled wood. The area was also mined for copper, and the remains of the copper mine can be seen from the well-maintained logging road that rings the lake. The community of Honeymoon Bay, adjacent to the campground, is named after two early settlers, Henry and Edith March, who spent their honeymoon here. Prior to the immigration of European settlers, Coast Salish people lived here, hunting and fishing in the region.

Location

Gordon Bay Provincial Park is on the southern shore of Lake Cowichan, 35 kilometres west of Duncan and 14 kilometres west of the town of Lake Cowichan. You can get to it by taking Highway 18 just north of Duncan.

Facilities

Situated in an area of second-growth Douglas fir, this campground has 130 large, well-laid-out camping spots. Those numbered 1 to 14 are closest to the bay and are separated from the main camping area (and the showers) by a quiet road. If you want to be near the waters of the lake and do not mind a walk to the showers, these are the better sites. There are flush and pit toilets, a sani-station, two shower blocks, and full disabled access. All spots are gravel, large enough to accommodate every type of recreational vehicle, and there are a number of double spots. Reservations are accepted and advisable as this campground can get very full.

Volunteer camp hosts work through the summer to provide campers with details of the area and information on activities and other campgrounds. The nearby community of Lake Cowichan has restaurants, accommodation, food stores, gas, a pub, and most amenities. Honeymoon Bay, just a couple of kilometres from the campground, has a good general store.

Recreational activities

Hiking

A number of trails lead through the park over a forest floor covered with thimbleberry, salal, salmonberry, and in the spring, wonderful wild flowers. (Remember, picking vegetation in B.C. parks is prohibited.) The Point Trail leads from the beach to an area of rock overlooking the lake. You can swim here, away from the crowds. Interpretative signs along the route explain the vegetation of the area. It takes about 30 minutes to complete this hike. Another trail leads from the parking area, through some yellow gates, and past a small lake onto the logging road that rims the lake. You wind up at a viewpoint from which the full beauty of Lake Cowichan can be seen (two hours return).

Boating

There is a boat launch in the park, and water-skiing is permitted on the lake. Lake Cowichan, one of Vancouver Island's largest lakes, is 32 kilometres long and 3 kilometres wide, with plenty of room for powerboats, jet-skiers, canoes, kayaks, and windsurfers. Boats can be rented in Honeymoon Bay.

Cycling

The paved roads of the campground allow pleasant, safe cycling excursions for the young.

Fishing

The fishing here is reputed to be excellent, as the lake has Dolly Varden, rainbow and cutthroat trout, chum, coho, and spring salmon for the angler. Fishing supplies are available in Honeymoon Bay.

Family activities

The biggest attraction is undoubtedly the wonderful sandy beach and large swimming area devoid of weeds or sharp stones. It is difficult to find a more perfect lakeside beach and although the waters may feel cold at first, they provide a respite from the hot temperatures often experienced here. The swimming area is cordoned off by log booms.

There are numerous picnic tables on a grassed area adjacent to the beach. Many are under the shade of the trees, but you will need to arrive

*Gordon Bay on the shores of Lake Cowichan is located in one
of the warmest valleys on Vancouver Island.*

early if you want to reserve one. An adventure playground has been
constructed within the camping area, and interpretative programs take
place during the summer. When I stayed at Gordon Bay there was a
program entitled "Slippery Slimy Slugs," which sounded very appealing for
the younger camper.

Activities adjacent to the park

After you've enjoyed the beauty of the park, you can partake in the activities
available in the surrounding area. A small museum at Saywell Park in Lake
Cowichan offers details of local history. Those who want a broader picture
can take a tour of the Earth Satellite Station. The Cowichan River meanders
through the community, and it is possible to fish for trout in its waters. A
disused wooden railway bridge is a novel way to cross the river.

The town's pub boasts the largest collection of miniature trains in
B.C. And has a strong train theme. Even the women's washroom is adorned
with a "Notice to Enginemen," telling all visitors how to start an engine
on a cold, frosty day. The pub serves delicious food and has an outside
patio with views of the lake.

The logging roads adjacent to the campground often attract trail bikers
Fortunately they are not audible from the campground. One logging road
that circles the lake offers an interesting excursion with good views. The
road takes travellers past the community of Caycuse, which until recently
was the longest operating logging camp in Canada—it started up in 1927.
Attempts are currently being made to preserve the location as a heritage
site.

Summary

Gordon Bay is a delightful, family-oriented camping location equipped with
all amenities, but be warned: it is one of the most popular campgrounds

on southern Vancouver Island and is frequently full. While it is primarily a campground for families, the fishing and boating facilities and the nearby community of Cowichan Lake make it just as attractive to adults travelling without children, especially if these adults choose to visit in September or May when children are in school.

My last stay was mid-week in early June, when only half of the camping spots were open and the BC Parks staff was just gearing up for the peak season. At this time my partner and I shared the beach with three other couples. We could see only two boats on the lake and were the only people brave enough to swim in the cold waters. This experience was in sharp contrast to my previous attempt to enjoy the facilities of Gordon Bay one weekday in August, when I was informed there was a three-day wait for a camping spot. Gordon Bay deserves to be one of the most popular family camping spots on Vancouver Island.

2. Sasquatch Provincial Park

Any first-time visitor to this provincial park cannot help but be in awe of the area's stunning scenery. As it travels the final stretch from Harrison Hot Springs to the gates of the campground, the paved road twists and turns along the edge of Harrison Lake. If you decide to holiday here, your vacation starts well before you reach the campground. Upon arrival, keep an eye out for the mythical Sasquatch, also known as Bigfoot, that is reputed to prowl around the mountains and valleys of the area.

History

The name "Sasquatch" is an English corruption of the Coast Salish word *Sasqac*. The Sasqac is a mythical creature, half man and half beast, that should be avoided. Local native bands still report sightings of the Sasquatch around Harrison River, so be warned!

The area is famous for its hot springs, and Harrison calls itself "The Spa of Canada." The therapeutic waters were first revered as a healing place by the Coast Salish people. Europeans discovered them in 1859 when a pioneer fell out of his canoe into Harrison Lake and instead of perishing in cold waters, found the lake to be warm. Development started in 1885 when a hotel and bathhouse were built. The water rights to the hot mineral waters are still held by the Harrison Hot Springs Hotel.

Harrison Lake is over 60 kilometres long, the largest body of fresh water in southwestern B.C., and is fed by the glaciers of the Coast Mountains north of Pemberton. In the 1850s it was on the goldrush route for prospectors travelling between the Fraser River and the gold fields in the Cariboo. At the end of the last century, logging started around the lake and is still the main local industry. Huge logging trucks are a regular feature on the roads. Today, Harrison Hot Springs attracts

From Sasquatch, you can see the ever-changing mountains on British Columbia's coast.

thousands of tourists throughout the year, but somehow manages to retain a quaint village atmosphere.

Location

It is easy to see why this park is such a popular family location as it contains four pristine lakes, including the freshwater fjord of massive Harrison Lake, and over 1220 hectares of land. It is a vast expanse to explore in the midst of beautiful mountain scenery. Sasquatch Provincial Park is located six kilometres north of Harrison Hot Springs. Take Highway 9 from the junction of Highway 7 to Harrison (6.5 kilometres), and then take Rockwell Drive to the park entrance. A good gravel road leads into the park and to the campgrounds, five kilometres from the park gate. Watch for logging trucks.

Facilities

In many respects, Sasquatch is not one provincial park but three, as there are three campgrounds here, all quite separate from each other, with a total of 177 spaces. Hicks Lake would be my third choice, as the camping spots are smaller than the ones found in most B.C. parks and some are very close together and regimented (spaces 18, 19, and 20, for example, are more like parking spaces than camping spots). Bench campground is near Deer Lake, although it does not have direct access to the lake. The spots are well situated in a forested area and there are a number of double spots. My favourite campground at Sasquatch is Lakeside, where a number of spots have direct access onto the lake. Even if you are not fortunate enough to obtain one of these perfect sites, all the others at this location are large and in a forested area.

All three campgrounds have flush and pit toilets, pumps for water, and there is a sani-station but no showers. The campgrounds are not wheelchair accessible. Group camping is available at Hicks Lake. The park accepts reservations and is very popular in the peak summer months. Services available in Harrison Hot Springs include a number of restaurants, coffee bars, shops, and boutiques.

Recreational activities

Hiking

There are two trails located near Hicks Lake. One is a four-kilometre hike around the lake. This trail may be muddy if the weather has been bad, but otherwise it is an ideal family hike. The other, Beaver Lodge Trail, is an easy 20-minute stroll around a small lake with a beaver lodge. Interpretative boards have been placed along the trail to explain the beavers' habitat and the fish spawning process. Lakeside Trail at Deer

As Sasquatch is located on the edge of Harrison Lake, the spectacular scenery begins before you reach the campground.

Lake is an easy, short walk to a lookout where you might see mountain goats on the nearby bluffs.

Boating

The four lakes at this location (Harrison, Hicks, Deer, and Trout) vary in size and in the recreational pursuits they offer. Harrison and Hicks permit powerboats, while at Deer Lake only electric motors are allowed. Powerboats are prohibited at Trout Lake, and consequently it is ideal for canoeing and kayaking. Boaters should be careful of deadheads and of the winds that tend to develop on the larger lakes.

Cycling

The gravel roads that lead to the three camping locations are ideal for mountain biking, and the roads and trails in all campgrounds are safe for children to cycle around.

Fishing

Trout fishing is reputed to be excellent, and you might also catch kokanee in the lakes. In addition to lake fishing, you can try your luck in the waters of the Harrison and Fraser Rivers.

Family activities

With four lakes to choose from, swimming here is delightful. Two beach locations at Hicks Lake ensure sun-worshipping opportunities; one is at the southern end and one by the group camping area. From this second location it is possible to swim to two small, forested islands ideal for exploring. There is a small beach and large grassy area leading to the waters of Deer Lake and there is also a jetty to sunbathe on.

A play area for children is located at the Lakeside campground, and interpretative programs are offered during the months of June, July, and August. The nearby town of Harrison Hot Springs is famous for its mineral pools and for its annual sandcastle building contest in September (see below).

Activities adjacent to the park

The quaint community of Harrison is a lovely place to wander. There is a beach area and you can arrange excursions on the lake through the summer months. More adventurous campers can windsurf, water-ski, or jet-ski.

A 20-minute return lakeside trail takes you to an edifice containing the emerging hot springs—you can put your hand in and feel the waters. This building is in need of renovation, so do not expect a photo opportunity. To truly experience the therapeutic waters you must book into the Harrison Hot Springs Hotel or visit the local swimming pool (the cheaper alternative). The public pool rents lockers, towels, and swimsuits and is open seven days a week. I advise anyone who has not experienced hot pools to try them, but don't expect to want to do much afterwards other than sleep; hot springs have a very soporific effect.

Each year, Harrison Hot Springs holds a sand-sculpture competition, with entrants from all over the world. Sand sculptures in the shape of Elvis, castles, loggers, mythical creatures, and more are on show from mid-September until mid-October.

Summary

Sasquatch is a super place for family camping and is a provincial park where, if the weather is good, it is easy to spend a week's vacation. While there are not a lot of hiking trails, if your family enjoys swimming, sunbathing, fishing, boating, or just having fun among fantastic scenery, then Sasquatch is a real gem. Its easy access to the town of Harrison Hot Springs means campers should not be at a loss for things to do even if the weather is inclement. Though it may be cold in the tent, the knowledge that hot mineral pools are only a 20-minute drive away will keep all visitors, whatever their age, happy relaxed campers.

3. Cultus Lake Provincial Park

While researching this book, I met a BC Parks staff member who went to great lengths to explain all the recent developments that had taken place at Cultus Lake. These included thinning trees, constructing riding trails, building a new reception centre at the park entrance, replacing vegetation, and reseeding the grass. This investment has no doubt taken place in response to the demands of the large number of campers who regularly choose Cultus Lake as their holiday destination. In 1995, the 28,500 camping parties who stayed at Cultus Lake made it the fourth most popular camping ground in the province. But I cannot tell a lie: Cultus Lake is not my cup of tea as I find it too large and popular. However, the fact that it is so popular means it does appeal to others, and if I had children or a boat my views would probably be different. Don't let me dissuade you from visiting and enjoying the BC Parks improvements.

History

The 656-hectare park encompasses both the east and west sides of five-kilometre-long Cultus Lake, from which a spectacular vista of mountains can be seen. The local Coast Salish people knew Cultus Lake as *Swee-ehl-chah* or *Tsowallie*, meaning "to disappear." The word "cultus" derives from the word *kul*, meaning "worthless" or "bad" in the Chinook language. Legends tell of a Slellacum or supernatural being that took the form of a huge bear and roamed the area around the lake. This Slellacum was believed to be responsible for the turbulent storms that could quickly develop on the waters. Consequently, the local native people avoided the area for centuries. Today, the crowds that regularly flock to Cultus Lake, and the

Jayne researching at Cultus Lake.

easily accessible commercial facilities that have sprung up, suggest many have found the lake anything but worthless, and the legends of giant bears have been permanently laid to rest.

Location

Set among forest-clad mountains, Cultus Lake Provincial Park is located southwest of Chilliwack off Highway 1 on a paved access road. Near Chilliwack follow the signs from Highway 1. Upon reaching Vedder Road, turn south and travel 13 kilometres to the park. From central Vancouver, if you don't encounter traffic problems, you can reach Cultus Lake in two hours.

Facilities

This campground is the third largest in the province (after Manning and Golden Ears) with 297 spaces in four locations. When you arrive at Cultus Lake, you will see a BC Parks reception building where you can get information on reserved and available camping spaces. The first campground you reach, Entrance Bay, is at the eastern end of the lake across the road from Jade Bay and the boat launch. A swimming area is located across the main road, within a five-minute stroll from the campground. Some spots are near the road, so traffic is audible, but all are in a forested area. Delta Grove Campground is my personal favourite, as about 18 of the 52 sites overlook the lake and are away from the road. Most sites are large and set amongst trees. Clear Creek Campground is across the road from the lake and offers a variety of shapes and sizes of camping sites, some with tent pads, some unsuitable for large RVs, and some close to the road. The most westerly campground is Maple Bay. This is also the most open of the campgrounds and is more sparsely wooded than the other three. Some of the locations here overlook the golf course, so this site is ideal for the golfing camper.

There is a convenience store on Lindell Beach Road, which runs through the Maple Bay campground. The campground host is also located in Maple Bay. All four campgrounds accept reservations and are equipped with flush toilets and showers. A sani-station is located at Maple Bay and the park is wheelchair accessible. You can find all necessary services within five kilometres of the park.

Recreational activities

Hiking

The trails in this provincial park do not challenge the serious hiker, but there are a number of short walks the family can enjoy. The most popular one is Teapot Hill, a five-kilometre round trip, steep in parts, but leading to views of Cultus Lake and the Columbia Valley. The Seven Sisters Trail

Cultus Lake is a very large and popular campground close to Vancouver.

connects Entrance Bay and Clear Creek campgrounds (two hours return). A third option is to hike from the eastern entrance of the park on Emerston Road and then take the horse trail. This horse trail was extended in 1997 with the help of the Vedder Back Country Riders and now emerges near the Maple Bay campground (three hours one way).

In addition to these walks there are two nature trails. One starts just west of Delta Grove campground and leads to a giant Douglas fir. The other is an interpretative trail near Maple Bay campground. BC Parks produces a leaflet with a map of the park that shows these trails.

Horseback riding
As mentioned above, a horse trail runs through the park. You cannot rent horses in the park but can make arrangements with riding stables close to the campground.

Boating
Boating is one of the main activities that draws people here. There are two boat launches in the park at Maple and Jade Bays. Winds can develop quickly on the lake, so be cautious. You can rent jet-skis, canoes, and boats from commercial outlets near the park.

Cycling
The ribbon of gravel roads in all the campgrounds ensures that young ones can enjoy cycling close to their campsite.

Fishing

Cultus Lake contains rainbow trout, cutthroat trout, and Dolly Varden. In addition, a number of rivers and lakes close by provide good fishing. The Chilliwack River is noted for steelhead as well as coho salmon and whitefish.

Family activities

BC Parks has a full schedule of interpretative programs. When I last visited, the daily program included events titled: "Boats, Bait or Binoculars: Tips on what to do," "Stop! Who Goes There? Campground Critters in BC Parks," "Walking in a Wetter Wonderland," and "Dwellers of the Wild." Jerry Rangers programs are organised twice daily to keep children entertained during even the most inclement weather.

The park is oriented for water sports with four beaches to choose from and safe swimming areas at Maple Bay, Honeymoon Bay, Spring Bay, and Entrance Bay. There is a children's play area at Entrance Bay campground.

Activities adjacent to the park

More than any other provincial park in southwestern B.C., Cultus Lake has a wide array of commercial facilities close to its boundary. These include go-carting, horse riding, boat rentals, swimming pools, waterslides, and golfing (golf courses are found at either end of the provincial park). Therefore, even if it is raining there is always something to do in the immediate vicinity. For those who require less commercialised activities, Chilliwack Lake, 42 kilometres east of Vedder Crossing, boasts a variety of pursuits among spectacular scenery (see Chapter 2).

Summary

While the setting and facilities here are picturesque, the park can become very busy during the summer months, especially on weekends, and very loud if too many powerboats and jet-skis congregate on the lake. Cultus Lake attracts a youthful crowd and many families who are anything but your overnight campers. The best time to visit the park if you want to avoid the crowds is in the spring when trees are budding, wild flowers blooming, and the woodlands alive with birds attracted to the deciduous forest. If your camping needs include all amenities and lots of activity, and if you do not mind large numbers of people, Cultus Lake at the height of summer is for you. To appreciate it at quieter times choose April, May, and September.

4. Porpoise Bay Provincial Park

I last visited Porpoise Bay in September 1997 and immediately felt something was different. My memories of Porpoise Bay conjured up pictures of family-friendly facilities, excellent services, beautiful scenery, a sandy beach, and a nearby town—just like the other family campgrounds in this chapter. I quickly discerned what had changed: a non-fire policy was in place and parks staff had removed all fire pits, giving each camping spot a slightly unfurnished appearance. A notice on the park's information board explained the decision: "BC Parks has responded to requests by the community and some campers to improve the air quality by reducing the number of fire pits in the park. At the same time, it is recognised that campfires are a special part of the camping experience. Dry firewood is provided at the communal fire pits each evening. The communal campfires offer children [and adults] the opportunity to roast a hot-dog or marshmallow and enjoy the experience of the campfire."

There is considerable debate about the use of open fires in provincial parks, and Porpoise Bay may be the forerunner of what could become province-wide policy. By encouraging interaction around a communal fire, however, this integral part of the camping experience will be maintained.

History

The original inhabitants of the area were the shíshálh people who hunted and fished in the region between the Strait of Georgia and Porpoise Bay. The name "Sechelt" is taken from this First Nation. In the eighteenth century, British and Spanish explorers roamed the coastline. The first European settler in Sechelt was Thomas J. Cook, who arrived in 1894. His daughter, Jean Whittaker, was born there in 1912 and still resides in the community.

Location

Porpoise Bay Provincial Park is on the Sunshine Coast, which stretches along the northeastern side of the Strait of Georgia between Howe Sound to the south and Desolation Sound to the north. To reach this campground from the Lower Mainland you will take an excursion on BC Ferries. Catch the ferry from Horseshoe Bay to Langdale, a 45-minute sailing, then follow Highway 101 to the centre of Sechelt, where paved, five-kilometre Porpoise Bay Road leads to the campground. The 61-hectare park is located on the east side of the Sechelt Inlet.

Facilities

Campers here want for nothing as Porpoise Bay has flush and pit toilets, showers, a sani-station, wheelchair access, and accepts reservations. There are 84 large, gravel camping spots, including a few double units in second-growth forest of Douglas fir, western red cedar, western hemlock, and alder. Fires are permitted in the three communal pits between 5:00 p.m. and 10:30 p.m. The campground has an area specifically designed for camping cyclists, which can accommodate up to 40 people. At the time of writing, the fee for these spots was $7.00 as opposed to $14.50.

Recreational activities

Hiking

A number of trails ribbon through the park. The most popular is the Angus Creek Trail, which leads to a tree-lined stream that is a spawning waterway for chum and coho salmon in the fall. Interpretative boards describe this process. Another trail leads to the marsh area of the inlet.

Boating

The park functions as a base for kayakers, who use it to explore the many coves and inlets of the surrounding area. Porpoise Bay is near the Sechelt Inlet Provincial Marine Recreational Area, which includes eight wilderness campsites located on the sheltered waters of the Sechelt Inlet—a paddler's delight. The area is also rich in marine life. Therefore, although Porpoise Bay is especially popular for families, those who choose to paddle away can find tranquillity amidst the West Coast scenery.

Fishing

When I last visited I saw numerous fish jumping out of the water only a stone's throw from the swimming area. Fishing in the inlet and the various rivers and streams can yield coho salmon and cod.

Wildlife observation

Porpoise Bay is recommended as a wildlife viewing location by the Ministry of Environment's BC Wildlife Watch program. You are likely to see loons, grebes, cormorants, ducks, and bald eagles. Information boards detail when each type of bird visits the park and your chances of seeing them.

Family activities

One of the biggest attractions here is the wide, sandy beach and the protected shallow swimming area ideal for young children. A grassy field with picnic tables, toilets, and change house is adjacent to the beach. From the sands, idlers can observe floatplanes taking off and landing at the other side of the inlet, providing an interesting distraction.

The park offers a number of Jerry Rangers and interpretative programs in the summer. These are held in a large, well-designed amphitheatre.

Activities adjacent to the park

The nearby bustling community of Sechelt is a pleasant place to explore. One of the most impressive buildings in the town is the House of hewhiwus

Porpoise Bay picnic shelters.

(House of Chiefs), a massive cultural centre containing the offices of the Sechelt Indian Government District as well as a museum, theatre, and gift shop. The staff members at Sechelt's Visitors Centre can give you advice on hiking, kayaking, fishing, diving, cycling, and golf in the area. You can take a lovely quiet drive up the Sunshine Coast north of Sechelt. Skookumchuck Narrows Provincial Park, at the north end of the Sechelt Peninsula, is well worth a visit, especially if you plan your arrival to coincide with the peak tidal flows.

Summary

Porpoise Bay is an excellent family campground, close to all amenities. Kids can have fun on some beautiful sandy shoreline. This campground is not only for the young, however. The Sechelt Inlet offers paddling opportunities and is a magnet for kayakers, while cyclists are well cared for in the cyclists' campground. One other advantage is the weather. The area enjoys dry, sunny, and moderately warm temperatures (average July temperature is 18 degrees Celsius) and mild winters with considerably less rain than the Lower Mainland, another reason to select this campground for a perfect family vacation. Others have also recognised its advantages, so you should make reservations if you plan to camp in July or August.

5. Rolley Lake Provincial Park

Some parks are criticised for being too big, some for being too small. In my opinion, Rolley Lake is a perfect size. It is also easily accessible from Vancouver, has a delightful setting, boasts a number of recreational activities, and is well equipped to provide an unforgettable camping adventure. Finally, Rolley Lake reminds me of the setting for Robert Redford's film *A River Runs Through It*, which is the story of two brothers and their father who enjoy fly-fishing. The last time I visited there was one lonely soul all by himself in the centre of the lake, fishing in a float tube, a big inner-tube contraption that anglers use. He demonstrated the same skills I had seen in the movie, but from a trickier position—sitting in the water as opposed to standing by it. I have never fly-fished, but as I watched this tranquil scene first thing on a Tuesday morning in late June I began to wonder how much it cost to buy fly-fishing equipment (and a float tube). My calm was disturbed by two chattering women in their fifties who were struggling to the water's edge with fishing rods, tackle boxes, coolers, folding chairs, cushions, and three young children. When I engaged them in conversation, I learned they had been friends for years, lived just down the road, and regularly arranged to meet at Rolley Lake so their grandchildren could have a fun time and they could have a good gossip and fish "away from the men." B.C. parks are not only for the camping fraternity.

History

Rolley Lake takes its name from Fanny and James Rolley, who settled here in 1888. In the early years of the century the lake was a storage place for shingle bolts destined for a mill at Ruskin, five kilometres away. In the 1930s, when all the old-growth forest was gone, the lake became home to a small Japanese-Canadian logging operation harvesting Douglas fir. BC Parks acquired it on February 3, 1961 (making it the same age as the author—I know which is wearing the best).

Rolley Lake is the perfect size and easily accessible from Vancouver.

Location

The 115 hectares of Rolley Lake Provincial Park are a relaxing environment for campers. The lake is surrounded by forest, with views of the surrounding hills. Rolley Lake is located 23 kilometres northwest of Mission (70 kilometres east of Vancouver). Although the 11-kilometre drive to the campground is well signposted from Highway 7, it can be confusing to find. In Maple Ridge, turn north off Highway 7 at 287th onto the Dewdney Trunk Road, turn right onto Bell Road, and then make a left turn towards the park. The road is paved all the way to the park gates, and a good gravel road leads to the camping and day-use areas.

Facilities

This popular campground has 64 spacious units set in a woodland area of western hemlock and mature vine maple that affords privacy and shade. There are a number of double camping spots, ideal for combined family camping excursions. The facilities are among the best provided by BC Parks and include showers, sani-station, flush and pit toilets, and wheelchair access. Reservations are accepted. Park hosts are on duty throughout the summer. Maple Ridge and Mission both have comprehensive services and there is a General Store, well worth a photograph even if you have not run out of supplies, six kilometres west on Dewdney Trunk Road.

Recreational activities

Hiking

There are a number of short walks in this park. The main one circles the lake and takes between 60 and 90 minutes to complete. It includes a section of boardwalk and leads through a forest where hikers can observe evidence of the area's logging history. The Falls Trail is a 20-minute return excursion leading from the campground to some broad, although not very high, waterfalls. This trail can be muddy in places if the weather has been inclement. Both trails have minimal elevation gains and children can walk them easily. You will find other trails adjacent to the park (see "Activities adjacent to the park").

Boating

Powerboats are not permitted so canoers and rowers (not to mention fishermen in float rings) can really appreciate the lake's tranquillity.

Cycling

The gravel roads in the campground are a safe cycling environment for young children, while the twisty, turning backroads of the surrounding area make pleasant cycling for older biking enthusiasts. Try cycling to Stave Lake, only five kilometres away.

Fishing

As mentioned, fishing is very popular here. The lake is stocked annually with rainbow and cutthroat trout, the main catch, while Dolly Varden and brown bullhead fishing is possible in the spring and fall. You can gain access to the water's edge from a number of places on the lakeside trail, and this is an ideal fishing spot for even the youngest angler.

Wildlife observation

Rolley Lake is a BC Wildlife Watch viewing site. Over 90 different species of birds have been identified here. Information on these birds and on your chances of spotting them is posted at the park entrance and on a notice board by the washrooms. You might also see deer, raccoons, river otters, and even the northern flying squirrel.

Family activities

Rolley Lake has a lovely beach and a large grassed area ideal for sunbathing and games. There are an abundance of picnic tables on the grassed area. The beach runs down to the clear, weed-and-pebble-free waters of the lake. When I last visited, the only drawback to this setting was the presence of a number of Canada geese who had also decided to holiday at the lakeside and had left evidence of their visit. Gingerly picking your way to the water's edge, trying to avoid goose droppings, is not everyone's idea of fun.

There is a play area in the campground, and during the summer months BC Parks offers interpretative programs.

Activities adjacent to the park

Two dams are located within a few kilometres of the park, Ruskin Dam and Stave Dam. Stave Dam, five kilometres northeast on Dewdney Trunk Road, is a recreational area with trails, a beach, swimming, and fishing. Just south of Stave Falls is the Hayward Lake Reservoir Recreational Area, which also has trails and swimming potential.

The nearby community of Mission is named after a Roman Catholic mission that was built in 1861 overlooking the river. The town was incorporated in 1892. Today it is a vibrant place that promotes itself as the "Shake and Shingle Capital of the World."

Summary

It takes less than an hour to reach this camping haven from my home in East Vancouver, so for anyone living in the Lower Mainland, cries of "Are we there yet?" should be kept to a minimum. Rolley Lake fish grow fat on the abundant flies and insects found here at certain times of the year, and there are a number of areas of stagnant water in the park (fortunately few in the campground itself), so make sure you remember the bug repellent.

Hiking is a favourite activity. You can take the boardwalk to the falls.

During my last visit I took a couple of guests from England who were visiting the province for the first time and who had arrived three days previously. They found it difficult to believe such beauty was at our doorstep and marvelled at the size of the banana slugs out in force on the trails. My visitors asked how often I had stayed here, and I felt embarrassed to say it was only twice in six years. "Why only twice?" they exclaimed. "If we lived so close to such beauty we would be here every weekend." Rolley Lake was their first introduction to B.C.'s parks, but their sentiments made me realise I had no excuse for not visiting more.

Additional Recommendations

The Best Hiking/Beach Campgrounds Those campgrounds recommended in Chapters 2 and 3, especially Manning, Golden Ears, Alice Lake, Rathtrevor, and Miracle Beach, all offer family camping possibilities.

Newcastle Island See Chapter 5.

Ruckle See Chapter 4.

Bamberton (Map reference 31) With 225 metres of beach looking over Finlayson Arm of Saanich Inlet a 30-minute drive from Victoria, this is a popular family location. There are 47 wooded camping spots and flush toilets, but no sani-station or showers. Reservations accepted.

Goldstream (Map reference 32) Nineteen kilometres northwest of Victoria on Highway 1, this large campground has space for 159 camping parties. Famous for its fall salmon run, the park also has fishing, hiking, and swimming potential. Reservations are accepted and facilities include showers, flush toilets, and interpretative programs.

Manning Park

THE BEST HIKING CAMPGROUNDS

Manning • Golden Ears • Strathcona
Alice Lake • Chilliwack Lake

The five campgrounds I have selected as the best for hiking include two of the most popular in the province: **Golden Ears** and **Manning Park**. Both have excellent camping and walking potential and it is possible to spend a week or more exploring each of them. **Strathcona**, on Vancouver Island, also boasts a wealth of trails and is quieter than either Manning or Golden Ears. **Alice Lake** provides the nearest developed camping to breathtaking Garibaldi Park, where you can see some of the best mountain scenery in existence. Finally, **Chilliwack Lake** has a number of diverse and interesting walks close to its boundaries, and unlike the other campgrounds listed in this section, is quieter, less popular, yet still within easy access of the Lower Mainland.

While I chose to include these sites under hiking, they are also family campgrounds with access to lakes and beaches for swimming, fishing, and boating. With the exception of Chilliwack Lake, all have interpretative programs throughout the summer months. These are campgrounds you can enjoy if you do not want to cover miles in a day but would rather pursue another pastime or just unwind.

As most of the parks in this section are at high elevations, some of the hikes are not free of snow until early July. Anyone planning a hiking/camping vacation prior to this time may want to check with the local BC Parks representative on the condition of the trails.

Some worthy hiking books to aid your choice of trails in the areas I cover here are: *Southern Vancouver Island Hiking Trails* by Fred Rogers; Jack Christie's *Whistler Outdoors Guide*; *109 Walks in British Columbia's Lower Mainland* and *103 Hikes in Southwestern British Columbia* both by Mary and David Macaree; Randy Stoltmann's *Hiking the Ancient Forests of BC and Washington;* and Jim Rutter's *Hiking Trails III: Central and Northern Vancouver Island and Quadra Island*.

6. Manning Provincial Park

Unlike many of Vancouver Island's provincial parks, which open in April with a season extending until October, summer activities in Manning are confined to the period between the end of May and September. I once stayed here during the Victoria Day weekend in late May, when cross-country skiing and snowshoeing were the most popular activities and only one trail was open for hiking. If you are planning a trip to this park early in the season, you may want to telephone the Visitors Centre to determine what facilities are open. While the sun could be shining in Vancouver, the snow may not have thawed here.

History

Manning Park is named after E.C. Manning, chief forester for British Columbia from 1935 to 1940, who died in a plane crash. It developed from the Three Brothers Mountain Reserve, created in 1931 to save the alpine meadows from overgrazing by mountain sheep. When the Hope-Princeton Highway opened to the public in 1945, Manning became a popular vacation spot with residents of the Lower Mainland and remains so today. In 1995 it was the second most popular campground in the province.

Its history dates back to the First Nations people who visited the area to hunt and fish. The present Skyline Trail was a well-used route for these early residents.

Location

The park covers over 65,000 hectares within the Cascade Mountains and encompasses two major river systems: the Skagit, which flows to the Pacific Ocean, and the Similkameen, which joins the Okanagan River to the east. It is within three hours' drive from Vancouver (224 kilometres) and is located on Highway 3, 30 kilometres east of Hope. The main park administrative centre is between Hope and Princeton. If you are travelling to Manning by car from Vancouver, take Route 7 instead of Route 1, as it is a far more scenic drive. Greyhound buslines operates a daily service from Vancouver to the park.

Facilities

There are four main campgrounds in the park with a total of 355 camping spaces: Hampton (99); Mule Deer (49); Coldspring (64); and Lightning Lake (143). At the present time, all spaces at Lightning Lake are reservable. This means campers who arrive without a reservation are restricted to using the three other campgrounds if Lightning Lake is full. Lightning Lake is the only campground with showers and flush toilets and is close to the beach, so it is the preferred camping location if you have young ones to

Heather Trail offers you a panoramic view as well as a floral carpet.

entertain or require the luxury of showers. A sani-station is located near the Visitors Centre. All the camping spots in the four campgrounds are large and private, located in a forested environment. Some at Coldspring and Mule Deer are near the water. Unfortunately, traffic noise is audible at Mule Deer, Coldspring, and Hampton.

In addition to the formal campgrounds, wilderness campsites are available in eight locations (open fires not permitted) and there is a group camping area. Manning Park Lodge provides lodge rooms, cabins, chalets, a licensed restaurant, a pub, a coffee bar, and a shop that sells a range of provisions for the camper as well as renting mountain bikes, canoes, kayaks, rowboats, snowshoes, and skis. When I visited, the Lodge offered to reimburse anyone who, after paying a camping fee, decided to take a break from camping and opted to stay at the Lodge—something to bear in mind if the rain starts pouring.

Recreational activities

Hiking
The first port of call for anyone visiting Manning should be the Visitors Centre, one kilometre east of Manning Park Lodge, to collect a detailed map of the area. Manning is a true hikers' paradise with over 276 kilometres of trails. There are self-guided nature trails, short easy walks (Engineers Loop, Rain Orchid, Twenty Minute Lake, Strawberry Flats, Dry Ridge, Viewpoint Trail), and much longer hikes. One of the most popular longer hikes is the Skyline Trail, which follows the north ridge to Lightning Lake with an elevation gain of 460 metres. For those who like a long walk without the up-hill climb, Lightning Lake Chain Trail is an easy 24-kilometre return hike along the sides of four lakes. When I last did this walk I saw

Lightning Lake Chain Trail is a 24-kilometre hike along the sides of four lakes.

deer, beaver, and grouse. Hiking the 21-kilometre Heather Trail in July and August is well worth the effort, as an array of over a hundred wild alpine flowers bloom in what BC Parks describes as "a floral carpet more than 24 kilometres in length and up to 5 kilometres in width." One advantage of this trail is that you make most of the elevation gain in a vehicle, leaving you ample energy to marvel at the views. I adore this walk and cannot recommend it too highly. The photographic opportunities are second to none.

Horseback riding
You can rent horses at Manning Park Corral and explore the four horse trails that range from 20 to 80 kilometres return. Horses are not allowed on the hiking trails.

Boating
Powerboats are prohibited in the park. Canoeing is a joy at Lightning Lake, where there is a car-top boat launch in the day-use area. As mentioned above, kayaks, canoes, and rowboats can be rented from the Lodge shop in July and August.

Cycling
You can rent standard mountain bikes and front suspension bikes from the boathouse at Lightning Lake. Mountain bikes are permitted on the 14-kilometre Windy Joe Trail and the 32-kilometre return Monument 83 Trail.

You may even find some snow fields as you hike.
They are so refreshing on a hot summer day.

Fishing

Anglers can fish for Dolly Varden, rainbow, and cutthroat trout in the Similkameen and Sumallo Rivers, while fly-fishers can try for rainbow trout in Lightning and Strike Lakes. Fishing licences are available at the front desk of Manning Park Lodge and tackle can be purchased from the resort store.

Wildlife observation

A wide variety of wildlife lives within the park, including over 190 different species of birds, which makes the area popular with ornithologists. It is not unusual to see black bears at the side of the road in the springtime. While a number of people are somewhat uneasy about sharing Manning Park with the resident bears, it should be noted that there has never been a bear attack in over 50 years of the park's existence.

Family activities

BC Parks staffpeople organise a number of activities specifically for children within the Jerry Rangers Program. They also offer informative, educational, and fun experiences for all the family on a daily basis throughout the summer months, with a series of visitor programs including walks, slide shows, puppet shows, nature paddles, and talks. Displays of the area's human and natural history are in the Visitors Centre, along with an abundance of other information. There is a small play area for children adjacent to Manning Park Lodge, and Lightning Lake has a beach and safe swimming area.

If you plan to be at Manning during early August, you are in for a treat. The park invites visitors to make floating lanterns, which they then cast out onto the waters of Lightning Lake at night. This family-oriented affair regularly attracts hundreds of spectators and lantern-makers and creates a magical ambience on the lake. Call the Visitors Centre ((250)840-8836) for the date of this year's event.

Activities adjacent to the park

The two towns on either side of Manning both have something to offer the visitor. Hope promotes itself as the "Chain Saw Capital of the World," with a rapidly expanding number of chain saw statues. It has a small museum and is a pleasant river town with all amenities.

When you travel from Manning to Hope, be sure to stop at the Hope Slide. A plaque and viewpoint indicate the area where, in January 1965, a side of Johnson Peak Mountain plunged into the valley, covering the highway with 45 metres of rubble. Also near Hope and not to be missed are the Kettle Valley railway tunnels. This is an impressive series of five large tunnels that were cut through the granite walls of the Coquihalla Canyon. Named after Shakespearean characters, they last saw railway traffic in 1959 and in 1986 were opened by the provincial Parks ministry as the Coquihalla Canyon Recreational Area. Visitors now walk through these tunnels to the sound of roaring waters below. The tunnels are signposted from the Coquihalla Highway and are well worth a visit.

Princeton lies 134 kilometres from Hope on the other side of Manning. Originally settled as a goldrush town, it has a small museum displaying pioneer artifacts.

Summary

If you love walking, Manning is the place for you, but be prepared to wait until the end of June to start the serious hiking. Because Manning is such a large park, it never feels crowded in spite of the high level of use, and it's a great place to holiday with your family. I particularly appreciate the facilities it offers. On those cold, wet mornings when you wake up and can't face the task of making a fire to cook breakfast with the wood sodden by last night's rain, it is a delight to know hot coffee and a cooked breakfast (not to mention a flushing toilet and washroom facilities) are only a few kilometres away at the Lodge. While this may not accord with the true camping spirit, even a seasoned camper appreciates some luxury.

7. Golden Ears Provincial Park

By writing a guidebook listing "the best," an author is exposed to immediate criticism, as what one person sees as the best may not be perceived that way by another. However, 38,202 camping parties visited Golden Ears in 1995, making it the most popular provincial park with camping facilities in B.C. I therefore feel pretty confident about including it in this book. Although I list this campground in the hiking section, I readily acknowledge that many visitors do not come to Golden Ears for the hiking but, rather, to appreciate some of the most beautiful and easily accessible scenery in the Lower Mainland.

History

There are two theories on how Golden Ears got its name. The first says it is named after the twin peaks of Mount Blanshard, which shine gold in the sunlight. The second says it was known as a nesting place for eagles—"Golden Eyries." Its history dates back thousands of years to the time when Interior Salish and Coast Salish people used the area around Alouette Lake as a hunting and fishing ground. During the early part of the twentieth century this was the primary site for B.C.'s logging activity. The main logging company was Abernethy and Lougheed, which ran the largest logging operation in the area, at one time employing over 1000 men. There are stories of the company sending a cross section of a red cedar measuring over three metres to England for the Empire Exhibition in the 1920s and of felling trees up to four metres in diameter. A huge fire devastated the area in 1931 and stopped the logging operations, although you can still see evidence of this industry today. The area was purchased by the provincial government in the 1930s as an extension of Garibaldi Provincial Park. In 1967 it was designated a park in its own right.

Location

Situated in the Coast Mountains between Pitt Lake to the west and Mount Judge Howay Recreational Area to the east, and dominated by the 1706-metre Golden Ears Mountain, this 55,000-hectare park is a short (45 to 60 minutes/48 kilometres) drive from Vancouver. It is located 11 kilometres north of Haney off Highway 7 on paved road access and stretches over 55 kilometres from its northern boundary with Garibaldi Park to its southern end.

Facilities

Alouette and Gold Creek are the two well-maintained campgrounds in Golden Ears. The former has 205 spaces, the latter 138. Both have large private spaces in wooded areas of Douglas fir, western red cedar, hemlock, and balsam. All facilities are present including showers, flush toilets, and a sani-station, and they are wheelchair accessible There are also two group campgrounds. Reservations are accepted and advisable if you plan to visit in the peak summer months or on weekends. A full range of services is available at Haney, while there are also a few small stores (and the delightful Black Sheep Pub) on the access road adjacent to the park.

Recreational activities

Hiking

To help you decide which of the many hiking and walking trails suits your needs, BC Parks has produced a pamphlet containing detailed descriptions. Trails range in length from easy hour-long strolls to the magnificent Golden Ears Trail (24 kilometres return), which takes a full day to complete and is best undertaken during the long daylight hours of July and August. Only the fit should attempt this hike, and I would also recommend you take copious quantities of bug repellent if venturing on this excursion.

For those seeking less arduous activity, there are a couple of short, self-guided nature trails at the southern end of Alouette Lake and near the Alouette Campground, while the longer Lower Falls Trail is particularly popular with families. The Alouette Lake Loop is a circular route around Mike Lake that takes about two to three hours and covers approximately six kilometres. If you want a climb, the Viking Creek Lookout is another alternative.

Horseback riding

The park is popular with horseback riders and there is an extensive system of trails. You can arrange riding excursions through stables in Maple Ridge.

Boating

Boat-launching ramps are available north of the day-use area and powerboats are permitted on the lake. During the summer months you can rent a canoe from the BC Parks staff and explore 18-kilometre-long Alouette Lake with its 30 kilometres of shoreline. This is reputed to be one of the best freshwater lakes in the Lower Mainland. Winds frequently develop around midday, so paddling is a more strenuous activity at this time. Canoeing allows you to explore some lovely quiet coves and escape from the crowds.

Cycling

Mountain bikes are only permitted on the park roads, Alouette Mountain Fire Access Road, and East Canyon Trail. There are negotiations underway to extend the number of mountain bike trails available in the park. The campgrounds themselves have a maze of paved roads that youngsters can explore by cycle.

Fishing

Even though the lake is stocked each year wiith rainbow and steelhead, the fishing here is not great, although rainbow trout, coastal cutthroat, kokanee, char, and Dolly Varden are found in Alouette Lake and River. Pitt Lake has a variety of fish and provides more diverse angling opportunities for cutthroat, rainbow, steelhead, Dolly Varden, and four salmon species in addition to carp, catfish, and sturgeon.

Family activities

Alouette Lake's numerous sandy beaches are a delight for children. The most popular is Campers Beach, situated between the two campgrounds. During the summer months, BC Parks offers interpretative programs on the natural and human history of the area, ensuring an educational and enjoyable experience for the entire family. There is also a playground.

Activities adjacent to the park

There are logging roads you can hike along in the University of British Columbia (UBC) research forest, less than six kilometres from the entrance to Golden Ears. There are also trails dotted with informative boards that give details of the forest's development and the fauna and flora of the area. When the trails in Golden Ears seem busy, walkers can be guaranteed tranquillity at the UBC research forest. I have hiked here on a number of occasions and rarely encountered another soul.

In the town of Maple Ridge, visitors can view the fully restored 1878 Haney House and one of B.C.'s oldest churches at 21299 River Road.

Summary

If you reside in the Lower Mainland and have children who ask "Are we there yet?" after less than ten minutes in a vehicle, Golden Ears is the ideal camping spot for you. With boating, swimming, walking, cycling, and an informative B.C. Parks staff there is lots to keep the whole team entertained. As mentioned above, the biggest advantage to Golden Ears is that it offers easy hiking into the coastal mountains with the luxury of civilisation only a short drive away. The biggest disadvantage is its popularity. Before the reservation system was put in place I heard of one man who regularly drove from his home in North Vancouver on Wednesday to book a camping spot for his family for the following five days. Then he would drive back home, leaving the spot vacant until Friday, when he headed out to the park again with his family. Urban legends like this make campers appreciate the reservation process, which was obviously devised to alleviate campers' mid-week stress levels.

8. Strathcona Provincial Park

It has been called "little Switzerland" because six of Vancouver Island's seven largest peaks are within its boundaries, as is the Island's last remaining icefield, Comox Glacier. Strathcona shares many characteristics with the other "monarchs" of B.C.'s provincial parks (e.g., Robson, Manning). It not only presents magnificent scenery, spectacular mountains, clear lakes, waterfalls, and forests, but there is also a Lodge just outside the park boundary with commercial facilities for those who decide not to camp or cook over an open fire, yet still desire to be surrounded by splendour.

Established in 1911, Strathcona is B.C.'s oldest provincial park and so is very much a monarch in its own right. It is home to Mount Golden Hinde, the highest mountain on Vancouver Island at 2200 metres, and Della Falls, the second highest waterfall in Canada, which cascades over 400 metres. Strathcona has an air of sophistication; this is a park for the adult population. While children will find ample to do, especially if the weather is good, it is those who recognize and appreciate splendid scenery and solitude who really adore this place.

History

Designations in Strathcona Provincial Park derive from native legends, early explorers, and entrepreneurs. The park itself is named after Donald Alexander Smith, First Baron Strathcona and Mount Royal, one of the principals involved with the construction of the Canadian Pacific Railway. On November 7, 1885, he drove the last iron stake into the railroad at Craigellachie in the Selkirk Mountains, physically uniting Canada and enabling rail travel from the Atlantic provinces to B.C.

The main body of water in the park is Buttle Lake, named after Commander John Buttle who explored the area in the 1860s, while the area known as Forbidden Plateau owes its name to Indian legend, which said the area was occupied by evil spirits that consumed women and children who dared to enter their realm.

Location

Set in a majestic wilderness encompassing more than 210,000 hectares of old-growth forest, mountain peaks, rivers, waterfalls, and lakes, Strathcona Provincial Park is located in the central part of Vancouver Island. Over half the park (122,500 hectares), including Big Den, Central Strathcona, and Comox Glacier, has been designated a nature conservancy area as it contains outstanding examples of the region's natural environment, unspoilt by human activities. No motorized transport is permitted here.

The main route to the park is Highway 28, which runs from Campbell River through the park and connects to Gold River on the west side of the Island. This is a pleasant, quiet drive and an interesting excursion even

Buttle Lake in Strathcona offers you views and reflections in every direction.

for those who do not plan to stay. In addition to this main route, there are two gravel access roads that enter the park from Courtenay. The first is a 26-kilometre road to Paradise Meadows; the second is a 19-kilometre drive to Forbidden Plateau. These roads don't go near the campgrounds, so be prepared for wilderness camping if you use them.

Facilities

Wilderness camping is permitted at least one kilometre from paved roads or in designated areas, but the primary camping spots are in two locations on Buttle Lake. Buttle Lake campground has 85 units and Ralph River has 76. Buttle Lake has the better beach and is therefore preferred by families, so it tends to fill up more quickly. Facilities at both these locations include pit toilets, wood, water, fire pits, and picnic tables. There are four marine backcountry camping areas on the west shore of Buttle Lake and one on Rainbow Island. There is no sani-station (the nearest one is at Elk Falls Provincial Park) nor disabled access, and fuel is not available in the park. However, all services are available in Campbell River or Courtenay.

As mentioned above, there is also a private Lodge just outside the park. It has an international reputation for outdoor education and operates a number of programs and courses as well as providing food, accommodation, and canoe/kayak rentals. The lodge has a dining room for evening meals, but the breakfasts are buffet-style, served at 7:30 a.m. sharp in a large canteen with long wooden benches. Fellow diners on these occasions can include fifty excited, chattering teenagers staying at the outdoor pursuit centre, dispelling any dreams of a quiet start to the day.

Buttle Lake is the main body of water in the park.

Recreational activities

Hiking

As you might expect, there is a great deal to see and do in Strathcona Park and it is easy to spend a week or longer hiking here. All walkers should pick up the informative brochure detailing the various walks. It is available from the kiosk at the park's eastern entrance, at the park headquarters, at the campground information boards, or from campground hosts. Most trails start in one of two areas: Buttle Lake or Forbidden Plateau. From here walkers can begin to appreciate the alpine splendour the region has to offer. At Buttle Lake, eight hiking trails take explorers on a variety of excursions ranging in length from 22 kilometres return to 6 kilometres return. There are also easy nature trails less than a kilometre in length. Forbidden Plateau is an area of subalpine wonder with a number of trails of varying lengths, some of which lead to views of glaciers, mountains, and on clear days, the mountains on the mainland. Access this area from Courtenay.

When deciding which trail to take, bear in mind the elevation gains and the time of year you are planning to hike. Many trails are under snow well into June, while some are inaccessible at certain times of the year. For example, the Della Falls Trail (with views of the world's eleventh highest waterfall) has a number of non-standard bridges, so when water levels are high the trail may be closed. This trails starts at the head of Great Central Lake and is accessed from Port Alberni by car and then boat.

On my last visit I hiked Phillips Ridge, which involved a three-hour uphill hike. At the top, I ate my sandwiches with what seemed to be the

View from one of the hiking trails in Strathcona Provincial Park.
(Courtesy BC Parks)

entire insect population of Vancouver Island before starting the descent. Previously my hiking excursions had included Upper Myra Falls and Bedwell Lake (this trail starts at the end of a seven-kilometre drive along a logging road). These were more enjoyable.

Boating

Those attempting to navigate the waters of Buttle Lake should be aware that it is an area of flooded forest. As a result, there are a number of deadheads and submerged stumps in the lake, particularly close to the shore. You should also be prepared for sudden strong winds and storm conditions that frequently develop on the water. There are two boat launches—one is near the Buttle Lake campground; the other is just north of the Ralph River campground. Water-skiing is permitted on the lake. You can rent canoes and kayaks from the Lodge.

Fishing

A wealth of streams, rivers, and lakes provide angling opportunities. Buttle Lake has good fishing for cutthroat trout, rainbow trout, char, and Dolly Varden, with the best fishing to be had from April to June and September to October. Fishing licences are available at the Lodge.

Wildlife observation

There are many wildlife viewing opportunities here as the park is home to large populations of deer and Roosevelt elk. Bears are also often seen in the area. Interestingly, the wildlife populations in the park (and on

Vancouver Island) differ from those on the mainland, and chipmunks, rabbits, coyotes, foxes, and moose are not found in Strathcona.

Family activities

This provincial park is a hikers' paradise and I have the impression it is not strongly oriented to family camping, especially as the weather can be changeable. Nevertheless, there are a number of activities and facilities to keep the younger camper entertained: swimming at both the Buttle Lake and Ralph River campgrounds, wide sandy beaches, an adventure playground at Buttle Lake, and a range of interpretative programs at both camping locations in July and August, details of which can be found at the campground notice board or at the park headquarters. The Lodge also provides some family-based programs. Westmin Mines is located in Strathcona and offers tours of its facility during weekdays in the summer.

Activities adjacent to the park

Campbell River is known as the salmon capital of the world, and literally thousands of anglers descend on the town each year to try out their angling talents. Ten years ago the town built a 180-metre-long, 6.6-metre-wide fishing pier that regularly draws a crowd of people ready to buy bait, rent a line, and try their luck. This is an ideal place to "people watch," even if you do not like fishing, and there is a lovely ice-cream store on the pier. The small town of Gold River, 89 kilometres west of Campbell River, has a nine-hole golf course and leisure centre.

Summary

Only 3 percent of Vancouver Island's population lives north of Campbell River. Perhaps this startling fact is the reason that, unlike many other provincial parks on the Island (e.g., Miracle Beach and Rathtrevor), Strathcona Park never seems to be too busy. It offers a more sedate, calmer camping experience, so is preferred by those who yearn for natural beauty and desire something more than sun, sea, and sand. This is a park for those who enjoy hiking and the outdoor life, and it definitely justifies more than one night's stay. The photographic opportunities are excellent.

9. Alice Lake Provincial Park

By including Alice Lake as one of the best hiking campgrounds, I may have stretched definitional boundaries a little as it is not so much this provincial park that affords hiking opportunities as the adjacent one, Garibaldi. However, Garibaldi only allows wilderness camping and is not easily accessible by vehicle, so Alice Lake, with its campground, is the preference. Many campers don't associate Alice Lake with hiking but view it as the perfect family campground. Whether your preference is hiking or just relaxing among the stunning mountain scenery, Alice Lake delivers the goods.

Its neighbour, Garibaldi Provincial Park, has a number of outstanding hikes leading to alpine meadows, glaciers, turbulent rivers, azure blue lakes, waterfalls, and mountain streams, encompassing some of the most breathtaking views anywhere. It sits within the Coast Mountain range and is home to peaks like Garibaldi Mountain (2678 metres) and Mount Sir Richard (2438 metres). Any outdoor enthusiast who enjoys strenuous walking during the day but also appreciates the knowledge that a hot shower and flushing toilet are not too far away cannot go wrong in selecting Alice Lake as a base from which to access and explore the magnificent scenery north of Squamish.

History

Alice Lake is close to the community of Brackendale, once larger than Squamish but now part of that municipality. Squamish, meaning "Mother of the Wind," has been settled since the late nineteenth century when pioneers from Europe arrived to log giant cedar and fir trees that were then tied together and floated across Howe Sound to the population centres farther south. Alice Lake was named after Alice Rose who, with her husband Charlie, was among the first settlers in the region. They built a homestead in the 1880s and earned a living by logging and farming. The provincial park was established in 1956.

Location

As mentioned above, Alice Lake is situated not far from the community of Brackendale, home to the largest population of bald eagles in North America. Visitors to this campground have a good chance of seeing these splendid birds, but they are not the only attraction in this extremely popular park. There are also four lakes: Alice (the largest, covering 11.5 hectares), Stump, Fawn, and Edith. The park is easily accessible from Vancouver on Highway 99—the Sea to Sky Highway—13 kilometres north of Squamish.

Facilities

The 88 large, private, shady camping spots are suitable for all camping vehicles and are situated in a forest of western hemlock. Paved roads ribbon through the campground, which is equipped with showers, flush and pit toilets, and a sani-station. Alice Lake offers disabled access and accepts reservations. There are a couple of small stores in Brackendale, and the growing community of Squamish has all services, while additional supplies can be found along the highway between Squamish and the park.

Alice Lake is only a 30-minute drive from Garibaldi Park and many hiking trails.

Recreational activities

Hiking

As mentioned, Alice Lake is a base from which to explore Garibaldi Provincial Park. Garibaldi covers almost 200,000 hectares and during the summer months you can hike to alpine meadows, glaciers, and mountains in the park. Much of Garibaldi (and the surrounding area) is forested with fir, hemlock, red cedar, and balsam. In summer it displays a breathtaking blanket of alpine flowers, making hikes in the area well worth the effort. You can obtain maps of Garibaldi Provincial Park, with details of the trails, at Alice Lake campground and from the campground host on duty in the summer. It is possible to spend over two weeks in the vicinity and still not explore all the trails. There are numerous entry points to Garibaldi Park, all within a 30-minute drive of Alice Lake. Five of the most popular entry points with trail access to the park are Diamond Head, Black Tusk/Garibaldi Lake (closest to Alice Lake), Cheakamus Lake, Singing Pass, and Wedgemount Lake.

For the less adventurous, there are a series of walking trails at Alice Lake itself. One of the most popular is the Four Lakes Trail, an easy, six-kilometre (two-hour) walk with minimal elevation gain that takes hikers around the four warm-water lakes that dominate the area. Interpretative boards posted on the section around Stump Lake describe the area's natural history. Numerous physical reminders of past logging operations

Walking trail at Alice Lake.

are clearly visible from the trail. Another trail leads up Debecks Hill. From here you have views of the area that was shaped by volcanic activity thousands of years ago.

Boating

All four lakes have paddling potential, with Alice Lake being the most popular site. Motorised crafts are prohibited on all lakes, which makes canoeing, kayaking, and fishing tranquil pursuits.

Cycling

A number of gravel roads that are attractive to mountain bikers run through the park. Some of the trails are closed to cyclists during the summer months, but are open at other times.

Fishing

At the southern end of Alice Lake there is a pier, popular with fishers, from which you can cast your line for cutthroat, rainbow trout, and Dolly Varden. The three other lakes also offer fishing possibilities. Edith, Stump, and Fawn Lakes are annually stocked with rainbow.

Family activities

As Alice Lake is close to Vancouver, it attracts a great number of Lower Mainland families during the summer months—and for good reason. It has beaches, a large grassy area for ballgames, numerous picnic tables, swimming, and sunbathing. Swimming areas are cordoned off from the open lake, and there are wooden rafts to swim to. BC Parks runs interpretative programs in the evenings and Jerry Rangers events for children during the daytime.

Activities adjacent to the park

In recent years the community of Squamish has grown in size and now boasts several attractions including a railway museum with a number of trains from a bygone age, some faithfully restored and others waiting to be returned to their former glory. One of the highlights of visiting this museum is the chance to speak to the volunteers and staff who tell interesting stories of the trains' previous lives. Squamish also has a golf course, a museum, and a number of commercial facilities that offer such things as helicopter tours of the nearby glaciers or white-water rafting excursions. The Tenderfoot Fish Hatchery is located just outside Brackendale and has exhibits of Chinook, coho, and steelhead.

Look back over Alice Lake and on to the mountains beyond.

Summary

Alice Lake is a very popular location, even during the week, and is frequently full over the peak summer months (in June 1997 it was impossible to reserve a camping spot for a weekend in July and August as all had been taken), so if you arrive during these times without a reservation, make sure you have a back-up plan. (One option is Nairn Falls Provincial Park, north of Whistler. It is not as popular as Alice, but also has developed camping—see Chapter 6). If you plan to spend time hiking in the area, check out some of the books mentioned in the introduction to this chapter as you plot your adventures. These, together with the information leaflets produced by BC Parks, will ensure the hiker sees some of the most spectacular scenery on the continent.

10. Chilliwack Lake Provincial Park

You are sitting in your Lower Mainland home and the weather report states the forecast for the weekend is hot and sunny, so you want to go camping but do not want to risk a long drive only to be turned away from a crowded site. My advice? Chilliwack Lake. Forty kilometres from the far more developed and commercialised Cultus Lake and accessible via generally good roads, this campground on the edge of a mountain-surrounded lake with waters as clear as glass is the ideal spot to spend a weekend. If you are a hiker there are at least four trails that will test your stamina. If you are an angler there is a massive lake. And if you just want to unwind, this is a beautiful, tranquil place to do it.

I last stayed during the Canada Day long weekend, and bad weather on the Friday made the crowds stay away. I woke on Saturday morning to brilliant sunshine and by the end of the day the campground was full (although there was still space in the overflow camping area). Though a number of campgrounds in the Lower Mainland are frequently full during the holiday periods, with a little bit of planning it is always possible to find your camping haven.

History

The name Chilliwack derives from the language of the local Halq'emeylem First Nation and means "backwater travelling." Early spellings included "Chillwayhook," "Chil-whey-uk," and "Chilwayook." Among the first European travellers to the region were British Royal Engineers who charted the Canada/United States border in 1860. Today a monument at Sapper Park, at the end of the lake opposite the campground, marks their exploits. The area has been the site of intensive logging, which continues today.

Location

Chilliwack and Cultus Lakes are signposted from Highway 1. The campground is located 64 kilometres southwest of Chilliwack. Take the well-signposted turnoff onto Chilliwack Lake Road, four kilometres south of Highway 1. This scenic 52-kilometre drive leads to the campground. The road is paved up to 6 kilometres from the campground, where a good gravel road begins. The road follows the white-water rapids of the Chilliwack River and I defy anyone to remain unimpressed by the grandeur of the surrounding scenery.

Facilities

There are 100 camping spots available in the 162-hectare park, and snowcapped mountains are visible from all of them. Sites 1 to 87, in areas named Lindeman Loop and Paleface Loop, are large, private, and well positioned. Approximately 10 have limited views of the lake, but my

Looking across Chilliwack Lake to the mountains.

personal favourites are those that look onto the large grassy meadow that also houses the adventure playground. Those numbered 88 to 100 have regimented parking but good areas for picnicking and cooking amongst trees. Only the basic services are provided (pit toilets, fire pits, picnic tables, water, wood). Reservations are not accepted. Should you find Chilliwack Lake filled to capacity, there are a number of BCFS campgrounds along Chilliwack Lake Road (see Chapter 7). The nearest concentration of services is in Chilliwack. A more limited range of provisions can be purchased at the Pointa Vista Store, 32 kilometres west of the park.

Recreational activities

Hiking

In addition to a collection of short trails that wind around the campground, a number of longer, tougher hiking trails are accessible from Chilliwack Lake. The information board at the park entrance describes some of these, as do the books recommended in the introduction to this chapter. From the Flora Lake Trailhead, half a kilometre east of the campground entrance, you can hike up 1000 metres to Flora Lake. Alternatively, a little farther along the same access road you can choose to travel 4 kilometres return to Lindeman Lake (well worth the climb if you are fit) or 10.5 kilometres return to Greendrop Lake. The BC Ministry of Forests describes this latter trail as "moderate," but after an intense uphill climb and a number of sections where I was hiking over scree, I found "moderate" to be an understatement. Having said that, I met one guy who was hiking up with his large rubber float tube strapped to his back. Some fishermen will go to any lengths for the elusive catch.

For those looking for an easy stroll, Chilliwack Lake Logging Road is a pleasant route to wander. A number of waterfalls crash to the road's edge and there are views of the lake and surrounding mountains. At the far end of the lake along this road is Chilliwack Lake Ecological Reserve (see below). You can undertake additional day hikes from the reserve through areas of majestic old-growth forest.

Boating
The park is equipped with a boat launch and every type of boat is permitted on the lake. One of the biggest disappointments during my last stay here was caused by two jet-skiers who made an incessant noise, easily audible from the campground well into what should have been the calm evening hours. Fortunately for those who have their own craft, the lake is large enough to escape this annoyance. Boaters need to be aware that there are deadheads close to the shore and that strong winds can sometimes whip up, creating waves and difficulties.

Cycling
The logging roads adjacent to the campground have mountain bike potential, while the gravel roads, trails, and grassy areas in the campground itself are a delight for cyclists of every age.

Fishing
The lake contains Dolly Varden, kokanee, rainbow trout, whitefish, and cutthroat trout, with the cutthroat and Dollys reaching up to 2.5 kilograms. In addition, you can fish the Chilliwack and Vedder Rivers and numerous small lakes and streams in the vicinity. Those who want to escape the powerboats and crowds often head to Lindemen Lake for trout fishing (fish as large as 30 to 45 centimetres) in its clear blue waters.

Family activities
This is a family-oriented campground and although there are no BC Parks-organised activities, children of every age should enjoy the facilities provided. There is a beach with access to the cold waters of the lake, which children seem more willing to endure than adults are. As the lake can become quite high, the beach is sometimes less than its usual 40 metres of sand in the early summer. The meadow is great for ballgames and volleyball, and there is a children's play area. Wildlife in the area (other than the excited children) includes coyotes, elk, black bear, and black-tailed deer. At Chilliwack Lake, children can have fun charging around the safe environment BC Parks provides, with little need for the formal rules that make up such an integral part of their other, urban lives. As I watch

Watch the weather over the mountains.

them, I am sure their memories of these camping excursions into the beautiful B.C. scenery can only be positive.

Activities adjacent to the park

As mentioned above, the Chilliwack River Ecological Reserve is almost eight kilometres from the campground down a logging road that follows the edge of Chilliwack Lake. It was created in 1981 to protect a unique area of old-growth forest featuring large western red cedars. A number of ecological reserves exist in British Columbia, geographically and biologically the most diverse province in the country. These reserves are areas chosen to preserve representative and special natural ecosystems, fauna, and flora, and are used primarily for scientific and educational purposes.

Chilliwack Hatchery is at the junction of Slesse Creek and Chilliwack River on Chilliwack Lake Road. Depending on the time of the year, you can observe chum, coho, Chinook, and steelhead here. The adventurous can go white-water rafting on Chilliwack River by arranging an excursion in Chilliwack. Finally, Chilliwack River Provincial Park is located 30 kilometres from Chilliwack Lake and has facilities for picnicking and fishing.

Summary

Chilliwack Lake allows easy access to some of the best scenery in the Lower Mainland. While relaxing by the campfire, basking in temperatures that can be in the high 20s Celsius, you only have to cast your eyes upwards to view mountain slopes, snow packs, waterfalls, and alpine meadows.

During the weekends of July and August, this campground attracts a number of young families (and dogs) that make noise while playing games, cycling, cooking, eating, and generally having fun. If you are banking on a tranquil location, my advice would be to look elsewhere. If, however, you are planning hiking trips during the week or in off-peak times, choose Chilliwack Lake.

Additional Recommendations

Nairn Falls See Chapter 6.

Pacific Rim National Park This park features one of the best-known hikes in British Columbia, the West Coast Trail. See Chapter 3.

Skagit Valley Provincial Park (Map reference 33) Bordering Manning Park, this 32,500-hectare provincial park is located in the Northern Cascades and has a number of hiking trails, some leading into Manning. Facilities include two campground sites providing 132 spaces with basic facilities (water, wood, pit toilets, picnic tables, fire pits).

Rathtrevor Beach

THE BEST BEACH CAMPGROUNDS

Pacific Rim • Rathtrevor Beach
Miracle Beach • French Beach

There is something magical about the sea. Whether the ocean is pounding or merely lapping on the shore, wave action is a sight we never seem to tire of. Water has a beauty by day and by night; constantly changing, it has the ability to simultaneously relax and stimulate. This chapter does not include beach campgrounds on lakes but is confined to those on salt water and, specifically, those on Vancouver Island. The selection is somewhat eclectic, as I attempt to present a diverse and intriguing choice of easily accessible camping adventures.

As you would expect in a chapter on the best beach campgrounds, I have included southwestern B.C.'s only national park, **Pacific Rim**. With kilometres of shoreline pounded by Pacific Ocean surf, it is the supreme beach park. Pacific Rim is also the only site for surfing in the region. For those who prefer more tranquil waters, two of Vancouver Island's most popular camping locations, **Rathtrevor Beach** and **Miracle Beach**, offer perfect family camping close to centres of population. Both are delightful vacation spots and are extremely busy during the summer, for obvious reasons. In contrast, **French Beach** is the place for a more adult-oriented camping adventure with its rugged, log-strewn beach from which, at certain times of the year, whales can be seen.

The views go on forever at Pacific Rim National Park.

11. Pacific Rim National Park

Campers who like beaches are in paradise at Pacific Rim National Park, which boasts an 11-kilometre-long stretch of surf-swept, sandy shoreline. There are three distinct areas that make up this 51,300-hectare (including 22,300 hectares of ocean) national park. In order to see all aspects, you would need to take two weeks or longer. The most famous area is probably the West Coast Trail, a rugged 77-kilometre excursion into West Coast rain forest, with wilderness camping provisions. You will need reservations if you plan to take this seven-day hike. Call (604) 663-6000 (Vancouver area), 1-800-663-8000 (rest of Canada and USA), or (250) 387-1642 (outside North America). The Broken Islands, over 100 islands in Barkley Sound, that also have wilderness camping spots, are the second distinctive feature of the park, while the third is Long Beach, with its fantastic sands backed by a dense barrier of rain forest, where developed camping is available.

History

The area's first inhabitants were the Nuu-chah-nulth (meaning "all along the mountains"), who the new immigrants knew as Nootka or Westcoast people. Many of the bays, coves, and beaches are named after the first European settlers, while the Wickaninnish Centre (see below) takes its name from a Clayoquot Sound chief who was frequently mentioned in the logs of maritime explorers and fur traders of the late eighteenth century. The West Coast Trail was cut between 1907 and 1912. There were a number of cabins along its length, and the trail and cabins were built to be used by sailors shipwrecked on the Island's west coast, who would have perished without this provision.

The national park was developed relatively recently. Before the dirt road between Port Alberni and the west coast was paved in the early 1970s, the area was not widely known except to Vancouver Islanders. The park was established in 1970, and the new road brought a flood of visitors. Pacific Rim is now a popular tourist destination receiving over 800,000 visitors a year.

Location

Pacific Rim National Park stretches for 105 kilometres along the west coast of Vancouver Island. It is approximately 120 kilometres from Port Alberni and is reached by travelling scenic Highway 4, which follows the rapid white waters of the Kennedy River.

Facilities

Developed, vehicle-accessible camping facilities are available in the Long Beach area of the park. (As mentioned above, wilderness camping is possible in other areas.) The main vehicle/tent campground is Green Point, with 94 spots located high above the beach. Here campers are lulled to sleep by the sound of the ocean. Facilities include a sani-station, flush and pit toilets, Visitors Centre, and limited disabled access. As Pacific Rim is a national park, a fee is charged for firewood. During the summer months, this campground is almost always full and consequently can seem a little crowded. In 1997, following a number of security problems, the walk-in campground at Schooner Cove was closed. Consequently, space at Green Point will be at a premium. Reservations are accepted at Green Point and to avoid disappointment you should take advantage of them. Services are available at Ucluelet and Tofino.

Recreational activities

Hiking

The Canadian Parks Service has produced a number of leaflets about Pacific Rim, including one listing the hiking trails. These leaflets can be obtained from the park information centre, or you can request them by writing to the park in advance of your visit (see the appendix for the address). Hiking excursions range in length from short trails with interpretative boards that describe the fauna and flora of the region, to day hikes and, of course, for the most committed, the 77-kilometre West Coast Trail. The Visitors Centre staff will recommend walks to accommodate individual time frames and preferences. One of the simplest, most pleasant hikes is a wander along the beach. You can walk along the beach and rocky headlands for 19 kilometres from Schooner Cove to Half Moon Bay, gazing out at the ocean to look for whales or staring up at the trees to spot bald eagles.

Boating

The area is popular with canoeists and kayakers. Businesses in Tofino and Ucluelet rent small craft and charter boats.

Wildlife observation

One of the biggest attractions here is the marine life, especially the Pacific grey whales. From late February to early May, as many as 20,000 of these creatures pass within sight of Vancouver Island on a 10,000-kilometre migration from Baja, California, up to Alaska. Some whales remain in the waters near Vancouver Island all year round. The Wickaninnish Centre has two observation decks with telescopes from which to view this spectacle (if you visit out of whale-watching season, the centre has videos and interesting exhibits of the local marine life). In addition, commercial outlets in Tofino and Ucluelet offer whale-watching excursions.

Other mammals of the area include killer whales, porpoises, sea lions, and seals, and almost 250 species of birds have been identified in the park, including bald eagles and ospreys that congregate in the rain forest leading to the beach. An estimated 10,000 Canada geese stop here during October and November—so watch your step if visiting then.

Family activities

Although the park cannot be described as family oriented, a beach the size of Long Beach obviously has a tremendous attraction for children. Surfers, windsurfers, swimmers, and kayakers demonstrate their skill for the entertainment of others, and the sands are perfect for beachcombing as the wild waves of the Pacific Ocean pound. This is invigorating in any season—as long as you have the correct attire. Be warned: the temperature of the ocean varies from 6 to 12 degrees Celsius, so it is very cold. After a full day at the beach, take in one of the interpretative programs offered at Green Point Theatre near the campground during the summer evenings.

Activities adjacent to the park

Beautifully situated at the entrance to Clayoquot Sound, the community of Tofino has seen considerable development recently and now serves as a centre for visitors touring the Pacific Rim. It has a number of cafes, restaurants, and gift shops, a museum/whale centre, and a wonderful art gallery. You can organise excursions by boat, floatplane, canoe, or kayak. One of the most popular trips is to Hot Springs Cove—Vancouver Island's only hot springs—which is 35 kilometres from town and is reached by boat or floatplane. At the cove, waters as hot as 50 degrees Celsius flow over a waterfall and through a series of pools to the sea.

The community of Ucluelet is less developed, but like Tofino has whale-watching excursions, craft shops, accommodation, and restaurants.

Summary

The park's setting is stunning. Roaring surf pounds a shoreline that stretches as far as the eye can see, while temperate rain forest serves as an impenetrable backdrop to this vista. Waking up and emerging from your tent or RV is an invigorating experience. Long Beach is an extremely popular camping location in the summer months, but it has just as many delights for those who choose to avoid the crowds and visit at cooler times. Precipitation is common; the region receives 300 centimetres of rain a year, so if you are visiting out of season, dress accordingly. You may wake to find the previous evening's ocean view obscured by a heavy morning mist, but this usually evaporates during the course of the day, allowing you once again to enjoy the sight as well as the sound of the ocean. Pacific Rim delivers a perfect beach-camping adventure.

12. Rathtrevor Beach Provincial Park

This is Vancouver Island's most popular provincial park and one of the most popular in the province. It regularly sees over 160,000 visitors per year. Within the camping fraternity, stories circulate of the impossibility of finding a camping spot here in July and August, with lines of RVs waiting to get in. Anyone who has seen the 2000 metres of beach and the first-rate camping facilities, including some of the largest, most private camping spots on the BC Parks roster, can easily understand its popularity. Rathtrevor is probably the perfect location (if the weather co-operates) for a family vacation.

History

Rathtrevor received its name from a gold prospector and pioneer, William Rath, who settled in the area with his wife and family in 1886. He died in 1903, leaving his wife with the farm and five children. To supplement her farming income she started to charge visitors for picnicking on her land. Soon picnicking led to camping and she charged a fee of 25 cents, then 50 cents per weekend (at press time the camping fee was $15.50 per night). Mrs. Rath eventually developed the land into a full campground and added the word "trevor" to the name for effect. BC Parks acquired Rathtrevor in 1967. The park started with 140 spots and four large parking areas and was expanded to 174 spaces in 1976. The Visitors Centre is located in the old family farmhouse.

Location

Rathtrevor Beach encompasses more than 347 hectares of land (including two kilometres of sandy shoreline) and is situated on Highway 19A, two kilometres south of Parksville (29 kilometres north of Nanaimo). It has views of the Strait of Georgia and the Coast Mountains on the mainland

Visitors Centre at Rathtrevor.

Rathtrevor's 2000 metres of beach await you.

beyond. Interpretative boards located on the beach indicate and name peaks in this mountain range.

Facilities

It is not only the sea and sand that attract campers to this location. The camping spots themselves are some of the best in the province. The 175 spacious sites are located in a forest of Douglas firs and accommodate every type of recreational vehicle. The vegetation is quite dense, affording privacy from even the nearest neighbour. The campground is fully equipped with a sani-station, showers, flush and pit toilets, and wheelchair accessibility. The washrooms are tiled and even have baby change facilities. A maze of paved roads with names such as Foam Flower Lane and Sea Blush Lane provides access to the sites. There are a number of double spots and group camping is also available. Reservations are accepted and advisable as the campground is *very* popular, especially during the months of July and August. A camp host is on hand during the summer with advice and information leaflets. Services are available in Parksville.

Recreational activities

Hiking

There are over four kilometres of easy hiking trails in the park, leading through the wooded area and along the beach edge. There are also self-guided nature trails. Some trails are closed to cyclists.

Boating

You can windsurf and canoe here, but there is no boat launch.

Cycling

Children adore this location for cycling. The paved roads in the camping area, and the many trails and quiet roads in the park, are a safe cycling haven to explore. The paved roads are also a delight for rollerbladers.

Wildlife observation

Bird watching is reputed to be good in the springtime and during the annual herring spawn.

Family activities

Famed for its beautiful sandy shingle leading to warm, clear waters, Rathtrevor is "unbeatable for swimming" according to BC Parks literature. This is the perfect family beach campground for picnicking and playing in the safe waters. Many families spend a week or longer just on the beach, which is well equipped with fresh water, a change house, and picnic tables. (Dogs are prohibited on the beach.) If you want to escape the crowds, you can find your own private beach spot on the waterfront closer to the campground, where there are more rocks and logs, but fewer people and less noise.

There are two children's play areas. In summer months the amphitheatre is used three times a day to deliver visitor programs like "Freddy the Frog," "Critter Olympics," and "Bee Social." The Visitors Centre, open 11:00 a.m. to 4:00 p.m. during the summer, has a first-class display of natural and human history artifacts including a display of live bees, stuffed

Rathtrevor's picnic area is beautiful. Stop and have a picnic or go for a beach stroll or a swim.

birds (including bald eagles, owls, and hawks), photographs showing the park's development and the logging history of the region, and marine life presentations. Staff members at this centre are keen to provide information about the animals and plants found in the park, in addition to offering advice on a multitude of other park-related issues. Each year in July the park hosts "Rath Farm Days" to celebrate the park's former life as a farm. Call (250) 248-3111 for the dates.

Activities adjacent to the park

There are a number of commercial facilities that have sprung up near the park. These include mini golf, go-carts, boat rentals, golf, water parks, and adventure play parks. The neighbouring community of Parksville is named after Nelson Park, one of the first settlers to the area, and offers a strip full of restaurants and fast-food stores. It also boasts a small museum and one of the Island's oldest churches, St Anne's Anglican Church, built in 1894.

Summary

This campground is extremely popular. However, if you arrive to find it full, you do not have far to travel to find alternative provincial park camping. Englishman River Falls Provincial Park is only 13 kilometres away and Little Qualicum Falls is 24 kilometres from Rathtrevor. I arrived at Rathtrevor at 10:00 p.m. on a Thursday in July, knowing it would be full but half hoping I could squeeze in. The helpful BC Parks staffperson informed me of space at Little Qualicum Falls and gave me directions. If you plan to stay at Rathtrevor in May or September, you will not have a problem. At these times the park's clientele changes as children are in school and the retired folk take to the road.

Although Rathtrevor is extremely busy, the number of people employed to administer the park's facilities ensures that amenities are well kept and well cared for. While the camper spends time relaxing on the beach, a platoon of workers empties the garbage, cleans bathrooms, rakes the gravel, and provides every type of help and assistance. One of these workers informed me it was like running a big hotel: you checked people in, ensured they were having a good time, gave them advice on where to go and what to see, and made sure the "room" was clean and safe. So why not go and book a week at one of the best outdoor beach hotels in the world?

Jayne, the happy camper, relaxing at the campfire.

13. Miracle Beach Provincial Park

With its wide sandy beach and views across the Strait of Georgia to the mainland mountains, it is easy to see why this campground is attractive to both adults and children, providing an ideal spot for a family beach vacation. In 1995 over 16,000 camping parties registered here, and when I stayed it appeared that children outnumbered adults ten to one—a quiet sunbath for the single woman was an elusive dream as children (and adults) raced around the sands looking for shells, clams, and lost family members. Like Rathrevor Beach, its proximity to large centres of population ensures there is plenty to do away from the campground if it does rain.

History

The area has been inhabited for millions of years. In 1988, fossilised remains of a dinosaur were found just south of the park. These remains of an "elasmosaur," a swimming reptile that measured four metres in length, were believed to be 800 million years old. The discovery was the most significant dinosaur find this side of the Rockies.

European immigrants began to populate the area at the turn of the century. They recognised the immense farming, mining, and fishing potential. One of the profitable fishing streams was Black Creek, which runs through the park. Miracle Beach allegedly got its name because two severe fires that devastated much of the surrounding forest narrowly missed it.

Location

The 135 hectares of Miracle Beach Provincial Park are adjacent to Elma Bay on the sheltered shores of the east coast of Vancouver Island, midway between Courtenay-Comox and Campbell River (131 kilometres north of Nanaimo). There are views of the Coast Mountains, and interpretative boards on the beach depict and identify the visible mountains, many of which are named after early European explorers. The park is situated just off Highway 19, and a paved access road carries you the two kilometres from the highway to the campground entrance.

Facilities

Miracle Beach has 193 large, private camping spots in second-growth forest of Douglas fir, hemlock, and western red cedar. In most campgrounds there are a few less desirable spots, but not here. These camping spaces are among the best BC Parks offers, and the vegetation makes them truly private. Paved roads named after the trees growing in the park wind through the campground, and it is only a five-minute stroll from your tent to the beach. All amenities are here including showers, flush and pit toilets, a sani-station, and disabled access. Reservations are accepted and advised if you want to camp in the peak of summer.

Nature House at Miracle Beach.

Recreational activities

Hiking

There are a few walking trails, an interpretative trail, and a dog-walking trail in the park.

Cycling

The paved roads of the campground, together with the trails, are a safe environment for even the smallest cyclist. When I last visited, cycling was a popular pastime for every age group.

Fishing

The best fishing is in October, when it is possible to fly-fish for coho from the beach mouth at the end of Black Creek. The town of Campbell River claims to be the salmon capital of the world and is a perfect place for the angling enthusiast to spend some time. It is estimated that 60 percent of visitors to Campbell River come for the fishing.

Family activities

Of course one of the main attractions is the lovely, long, sand and pebble beach, perfect for swimming and sunbathing. Numerous logs along the shoreline provide backrests and props where adults can sit and read while the children run off to the safe waters. The beach is equipped with a change house, picnic tables, and toilets. Dogs are prohibited. Low tide reveals rock pools to explore and there is a vast array of creatures and other objects for young and old beachcombing enthusiasts to discover.

To supplement personal beach and woodland investigations, the excellent Visitors Centre/Nature House has saltwater aquariums, displays of whales, fossils, butterflies, and bugs, and a live tarantula named Sly. BC

Parks staffpeople are on hand to offer information and run interpretative programs with appealing names such as "Jerry the Jellyfish" and "Slime Time." The place is a real hive of activity during the summer months. When I visited a display featuring a fire-bellied tree frog that was billed as "visiting from Australia." The cross section of a 300-year-old Douglas fir, 1.7 metres in diameter, is on show outside the centre. During the evening, programs for all the family are presented in the park amphitheatre.

Activities adjacent to the park

As the park is near two large centres of population (Campbell River, 19 kilometres to the north, and Courtenay-Comox, 24 kilometres to the south), there are a number of non-beach-related activities available. These include golfing, ferry trips to the islands of Quadra, Cortes, Hornby, and Denman, and boating and fishing excursions. There is a museum and archive in Courtenay, and to the west of the town is the Puntledge River Hatchery.

Campbell River has seen considerable redevelopment in recent years and now has a number of shops to visit and oceanfront paths. There is also a pier where you can rent fishing tackle and purchase ice cream.

Summary

Miracle Beach is not only perfect by day. At night there seem to be many more stars than you see in the city, and it is wonderful to sit on the beach and watch the sun go down. Although the beach here is not as large as Rathtrevor's to the south, these two campgrounds offer similar facilities, making it difficult to decide which one to select. Miracle Beach is smaller and slightly less developed than Rathtrevor and is also not quite as popular.

Miracle Beach begs you to take a short walk along its shore.

14. French Beach Provincial Park

This is a beach that means business. It is not a tidy, manicured beach with numerous lifeguards, wooden rafts, and a safe swimming area for children. Nor is it a beach with waves too scared to pound the sands or to reclaim the huge logs their waters deposited just a few hours previously. This is a rugged, pebbled, log-strung oceanfront with exceptional views across the Strait of Juan de Fuca to the Olympic Mountains in Washington State. Prone to mists, this camping facility can have an almost otherworldly feel, especially first thing in the morning, but when the fogs that envelop the landscape clear, the spectacular vista returns. Beaches by their very nature are romantic places, but French Beach does not provide a sanitised romantic experience. It is not the beach on the holiday poster with sparkling white sands and clear blue, gentle waters. Walking hand in hand along these sands involves navigating logs, rocks, tree roots, seaweed, and other ocean debris. It presents an untamed environment perfect to explore at any time of the year.

History

This coastline was explored in the eighteenth century by the Spanish, who were searching for gold. In 1849, Captain William Grant was given a contract by the Hudson's Bay Company to establish a farm in what is now the town of Sooke. He was soon enticed away to the gold fields of California. Other settlers subsequently came to the area but had limited success with farming. This century has seen the growth of the logging industry, and Sooke was initially, and to a limited extent still is today, a logging town. French Beach Provincial Park was established in 1974 and provides access to one of the many beaches along this stretch of the Strait of Juan de Fuca.

Location

The 59-hectare provincial park is located on twisting Highway 14, twenty kilometres west of Sooke. Beyond Sooke this road loses most of its traffic and follows the shoreline through forests, by fields, and over headlands, offering spectacular views of the Olympic Peninsula and the adjacent Pacific waters. The journey to the campground (and beyond) is a delight.

Facilities

Set in a forest of Douglas fir, Sitka spruce, western hemlock, and western red cedar are 69 large, shady camping spots suitable for every type of recreational vehicle. The park is wheelchair accessible and reservations are accepted. Some of the best spots are reservable and close to the ocean, and from many campsites you can listen to the waves on the shore. A paved road winds between the gravel camping spaces. There is a sani-station but only pit toilets. A small store near the campground sells supplies

French Beach is a rugged, log-strung oceanfront with exceptional views.

and propane, while full services are within easy reach at Sooke. The community of Jordan River, five kilometres west of the campground, has a quaint, inexpensive, licensed restaurant where you can eat breakfast, lunch, and dinner while you enjoy the mountain views over the Juan de Fuca Strait.

Recreational activities

Hiking

There are a couple of small hiking trails that lead through rain-forested land to the beach. Walking along the beach is wonderful.

Fishing

Sea fishing is possible. A couple of lakes in the vicinity have fresh-water fishing, including Bear Creek Reservoir, 15 kilometres northeast of Jordan River, where stocks of rainbow and cutthroat trout are released each year.

Wildlife observation

It is not unusual to see river otters, seals, and sea lions playing offshore, while ospreys and bald eagles frequent the skies overhead. Interpretative boards in the park describe some of the local wildlife.

One of the biggest attractions here is whale watching. Magnificent grey whales migrate to their feeding grounds in the spring and return in the fall. If you are lucky you can view them from the beach, or if you're an experienced paddler, at closer range in a kayak. Roaming pods of killer whales also pass by sometimes. A number of commercial outlets in Victoria,

Ucluelet, and Tofino on the west coast of Vancouver Island, and in Nanaimo on the east coast, offer whale-watching trips. Tour operators can give you an idea of your chances of seeing these splendid creatures.

Family activities
The campground has an adventure playground and youngsters can explore the gravel roads by bike. It is possible to swim in the sea, but the waves can be pretty powerful. Beachcombing is a delight as rock pools are revealed at low tide, exposing an array of shore life.

Activities adjacent to the park
Victoria is about an hour's drive from French Beach and presents a wealth of city-based activities including shopping, museums, gardens, an excellent Chinatown, and art galleries. For those who seek quieter alternatives, a number of possibilities are available on Highway 14. China Beach Provincial Park, west of French Beach, offers a 15-minute walk through rain forest to a beach with walking and beachcombing potential. Port Renfrew, at the end of Highway 14, is the start (or finish) of the famous West Coast Trail. It also is an access point for Botanical Beach, which attracts visitors from all over the world interested in its rich marine life. For those who do not want to return along Highway 14, a good gravel road leads from Port Renfrew to Lake Cowichan.

Summary
This provincial park's biggest draw is the huge beach. It's a beautiful place to sit and watch the sun go down or star gaze. I last stayed in late May when there were few other campers. After dinner my partner and I dressed in warm clothes to keep out the wind, and with blankets and flashlight in hand we walked down to the ocean. The beach was entirely ours. We selected our log and sat against it to watch the waves break, the skies darken, and the stars come out. Nothing interrupted our view of the night sky and there were shooting stars to watch. This magical vista lives in my memory as one of the best camping moments and confirms my view of French Beach as a place for couples who appreciate and are content with the simple pleasures of life.

Additional Recommendations
The Best Island Campgrounds All the recommendations in Chapter 4 have beaches to explore.
Sidney Spit, **Newcastle Island**, **Porteau Cove** See Chapter 5.
Bamberton (Map reference 31) With 225 metres of beach looking over Finlayson Arm of Saanich Inlet, and only a 30-minute drive from Victoria, this is a popular family location. There are 47 wooded camping spots and flush toilets but no sani-station or showers. Reservations accepted.

Pender Island

THE BEST ISLAND CAMPGROUNDS

Montague Harbour • Ruckle
Fillongley • Prior Centennial

There is something special about camping on an island. Island communities have a different feel about them. They seem more relaxed, less stressed, and in southwestern B.C. they have an almost bohemian atmosphere. Although they still live close to major centres of population, island inhabitants maintain an air of detachment and a different outlook on life. Many are artists, writers, and craftspeople who seek quality of life above material pursuits.

When you travel to the four Gulf Islands described below, it is as if you breathe a different air that lets you foster the same laid-back mentality as the island community. Do not consider camping here if you seek action and adventure; these are environments for total relaxation.

Journeying to and from Saltspring, Galiano, Denman, and Pender Islands involves a ride on BC Ferries, so when you plan your journey, remember to check sailing times. Ferry reservations are recommended. Phone (250) 386-3431 (Vancouver Island), (604) 277-0277 (Vancouver), or 1-888-223-3779 (everywhere else), or check the website at http://www.bcferries.bc.ca.

I describe four provincial park campgrounds in this chapter. **Montague Harbour** on Galiano is effectively a marine park but has wonderful camping facilities. **Ruckle** on Saltspring Island has space for the RV crowd but there are fantastic oceanfront facilities for those who choose to walk in to these sites. **Fillongley** on Denman Island has a beautiful beach among its many advantages, while **Prior Centennial** on North Pender is a base from which to explore country lanes. All these islands are attractive to cyclists, as the roads are quieter and more varied than those on the mainland.

15. Montague Harbour Provincial Marine Park

Two hours from downtown Vancouver or Victoria, a beautiful little campground waits to supply you with everything needed for a weekend escape from the city: calm sea waters, wide white beaches, shady camping spots, and a tranquillity that only an island can provide. I adore this place, but not for its natural beauty alone. My other reason for singing its praises relates to the bus service on Friday and Saturday nights that ferries campers and the visiting boating fraternity to and from the island's only pub. The Hummingbird Pub provides excellent food, live entertainment, and, of course, the odd alcoholic beverage. Secure in the knowledge that you will not be driving, the pub staff does its part to ensure a campground and marina full of happy folks. If you intend to visit during the summer months, be sure to reserve a spot or be prepared to search for alternative accommodation as Montague Harbour is a much-sought-after destination.

History

The island is named after Dionisio Alcala Galiano, commander of the *Sutil*, who explored the area and claimed the island for Spain in 1792. However, shell middens at Montague Harbour that are estimated to be over 3000 years old testify to the much earlier, semi-permanent settlement of the Coast Salish people in the area. There is an archaeological site in the park where spearheads, carvings, and arrows have been found.

One of the earliest European settlers on Galiano was a man named Henry Georgeson, who came from the Shetland Islands in the mid-1800s, purchased 59 hectares of land, and hunted deer. The people who settled on the island in the nineteenth century tended to build their homes at the south end of Galiano, near Whaler Bay, Sturdies Bay, and Georgeson Bay. Most of the island's 1000 inhabitants are still to be found in this area.

The twentieth century saw the development of a fishing industry. Herring was salted in five different places on Galiano; Japanese people ran four of the plants, while the fifth was a Chinese operation. A cannery and saltery were started on the island but closed just before World War II when the Japanese were interned and sent to the Interior of B.C. Today many artists and craftspeople have chosen to live here, and there are a few restaurants, craft shops, and a first-rate bakery in the area around Sturdies Bay.

Location

Montague Harbour is B.C.'s oldest marine park. When it opened in 1959 it was the first provincial park to serve visitors who arrived in their own boats as well as by car or on foot. The park encompasses an 89-hectare area that starts 5 metres below sea level and rises to 180 metres above. It includes a lagoon, a tidal salt marsh, a forest of various trees and undergrowth, a beach, cliffs, and rocks, and consequently is a varied and interesting place to explore or relax. If you do not have your own boat, you can reach Galiano Island via BC Ferries from Swartz Bay on Vancouver Island (about 45 minutes) or from Tsawwassen on the mainland (about 50 minutes). Then drive 10 kilometres from Sturdies Bay to the park.

Facilities

There are 40 well-positioned camping spots here: 25 are suitable for vehicles and are set in a forested area with Douglas fir, western hemlock, and western red cedar, while many of the 15 walk-in sites overlook the harbour and have better views than the drive-in units. The drive-in units are large and accommodate almost all sizes of recreational vehicles. Group camping is also available. Facilities are restricted to the basic ones found in BC Parks (pit toilets, wood, water, picnic tables, fire pits). There is no sani-station or disabled access. As mentioned above, reservations are accepted and advisable.

There are a number of bed and breakfasts, lodges, and cabins on the island, and another provincial park, Dionisio Point, in the north. Most services are at Sturdies Bay, including a grocery and general store, restaurants, and a bakery that not only supplies tasty baked goods but is also a great place to sit and drink coffee and watch the world go by. You can rent kayaks and bicycles in the village. The marina adjacent to the campground has a small store and coffee bar (when I stayed here, the coffee bar served freshly baked cinnamon buns first thing in the morning) where you can get some basic supplies.

Recreational activities

Hiking

There is one three-kilometre trail that follows the shoreline and lagoon around Gray Peninsula (named after Captain Gray, an early explorer who

Montague Harbour displays a natural beauty all its own.

Galiano Island is a favourite spot for boaters.

settled on the island and cultivated an orchard that supplied fruit to the people of Victoria), created by glacial action thousands of years ago. Other little trails zigzag their way around the campsites on the park's north side. Members of the local community have worked to create a number of hiking trails on the island and recommend tourists visit Bellhouse Provincial Park—described as possibly the most scenic park in the Gulf Islands— and hike to Bluffs Park and Mount Galiano. When I attempted this a couple of years ago, the signage left a lot to be desired, but the views of Active Pass were worth it. There are also trails along Bodega Ridge (at the north end of the island) and in Dionisio Point Provincial Park. This park has recently been closed to camping, but it offers an outstanding view over the Strait of Georgia towards Vancouver and an interesting coastline for exploration.

Boating
There is a boat launch in the park, and kayaks can be rented from the nearby marina and at Sturdies Bay. Kayaking is a good way to explore the coastal scenery and is safe, as the waters of the bay are generally calm.

Cycling
While there is little opportunity for cycling in the campground itself, Galiano has lovely, quiet roads, especially once you leave the main population centre. Be warned, however, that Galiano is not by any means flat! Bikes can be rented in Sturdies Bay. Cyclists can easily travel the length of the island on Porlier Pass Road. If you are cycling in the summer, you will find ice cream stores and cafes to refresh yourself en route.

Fishing
The area has abundant supplies of salmon and shellfish. This feature is not only appreciated by anglers, but also by the population of bald eagles and other birds that frequent the island.

Family activities

This provincial park is suitable for retired individuals with time on their hands and for families. The sandy, shell-covered beach and the clear, warm waters are perfect for swimming, beachcombing, and sunbathing, while the easy walks and trails within the park boundaries are alternative attractions.

The park's staff offers interpretative programs in the summer. They are held in a floating nature house. During evening events you might find yourself looking through the transparent floor of this structure into the ocean to see the sea life. The presenters give fascinating accounts of the creatures that can be viewed in this magical way. Reserve your spot in these programs by signing up on the BC Parks notice board.

Activities adjacent to the park

Montague Harbour is an ideal base from which to explore other Gulf Islands in your own craft or on BC Ferries. There are daily sailings to Mayne, Pender, Saturna, and Saltspring Islands. As previously mentioned, Sturdies Bay has a number of craft and art shops and hosts some summertime activities.

Summary

Galiano is smaller and less commercialised than Saltspring Island, but offers more amenities than Pender, and Montague Harbour is a park that can be appreciated by every age group. While I have attempted to describe the many activities available here, probably the best activity is to enjoy the scenery and unwind. As the park is relatively small, the beach is never crowded and you can spend many hours reading and relaxing by the calm waters. In the evening you can view breathtaking sunsets, and at night the heavens explode with an abundance of stars that fill a sky far bigger than what you see in Vancouver.

BC Ferries offers you a relaxing journey to any of the islands.

16. Ruckle Provincial Park

In 1974, the Ruckle family sold a 486-hectare parcel of land to the provincial government for a nominal fee. In so doing they gave the people of B.C. And visitors to the province a superb park and campground. If you want to camp in an RV or need to be near your vehicle while camping, the five-minute forest walk from the parking area to the campground overlooking the waters of Swanson Channel may deter you. For many, however, the views and tranquillity this waterfront location offers negate any problems in transportation. When I stayed, the trek from the car to our spot on the water's edge added to the fun of the camping experience. It seemed to do the same for others, including one couple that managed to successfully, although somewhat noisily, carry all their camping equipment, three children, and a dog to their chosen spot. "Travelling light" was not an expression that came to mind on this occasion.

History

The Cowichan people called Saltspring *Chu-an*, meaning "facing the sea." The name Saltspring came from the 14 briny pools on the north end of the island. The first European inhabitants of Saltspring Island were pioneers who arrived in the mid-nineteenth century with encouragement from James Douglas, the colonial governor of Victoria. They introduced farming to the island.

Among these pioneers were Henry Ruckle and his son Daniel, who settled in the southern area of the island and established a farmstead in 1872. This area is now the provincial park. The Ruckles' original home, constructed in the 1870s, together with two other homes built in 1908, can be seen on the property. A farmhouse constructed in the 1940s now

Ruckle offers you a chance to get away from it all. (Courtesy BC Parks)

serves as the park headquarters. This land was used continuously for farming from the late 1800s until today, which makes it one of B.C.'s oldest family farms. The Ruckle family retains its right to life tenancy within the park, and family members still live in the beautiful old houses and farm 80 hectares of land. Visitors can tour the historical farm buildings and learn of farming practices of a bygone age.

In contrast to this bucolic setting, nearby Beaver Point was an infamous rum-running port during the 1920s, when liquor smugglers did brisk business over the Canada-US border.

Location

The 486-hectare park is situated 12 kilometres from Fulford Harbour at Beaver Point (at the end of Beaver Point Road) on the southeastern corner of Saltspring Island. This is the largest park in the Gulf Islands, on the largest of the islands. As you drive to the park, watch for Fulford's picturesque church overlooking the harbour. It was built over a hundred years ago.

Facilities

As mentioned above, there are 70 walk-in camping spots in a grassy area that looks straight onto the waters of Swanson Channel. There is parking for RVs but no campsites immediately adjacent. The walk from the parking area to the campground takes under five minutes on level ground. Be careful when you transport equipment to the campsite from your vehicle as there are a number of crows adept at breaking into food bags and containers once your back is turned. All the basic amenities are found here (pit toilets, wood, water, picnic tables, fire pits), but there is no sani-station or disabled access. The nearest services can be found in the community of Fulford Harbour and include a grocery store, gas station, coffee bar, Mexican restaurant, ice cream parlour, pottery shop, and pub.

Recreational activities

Hiking

Ruckle Park has over seven kilometres of shoreline characterised by pocket beaches, rocky coves, and headlands waiting to be explored. A number of walking trails lead around the headlands and into the forested areas. Trails range in length from ten minutes to over two hours and provide access to the area's many bays and coves.

Cycling

The park is ideal for anyone who wants to explore by bicycle. Indeed, as the campground is only half an hour by bike from the ferry terminal, many campers arrive on quiet Beaver Point Road using this mode of transport.

There are a number of paved roads and tracks to explore, as one would expect in an area with a farming history.

Fishing

Stowell Lake and Western Lake are two good trout-fishing lakes about 10 kilometres from Ruckle on the road to Fulford Harbour. You can also swim at both these locations.

Wildlife observation

From your tent you can observe otters, harbour seals, porpoises, sea lions, and, if you are very fortunate, killer whales as they swim in the adjacent waters. BC Parks interpretive boards near the campground give information about these creatures. I saw sea lions and seals when I stayed, but no killer whales. It is hard to believe they travel into these waters, which are heavily used by BC Ferries, but it's true! The mixture of forest, field, and shoreline habitats makes Ruckle one of the most productive wildlife viewing areas and a magnet for ornithologists and naturalists.

Family activities

Although there are no specific activities for children, the vast expanse of Ruckle's grassy fields, forests, and shoreline makes it a delight for youngsters to explore. It is possible to swim, beachcomb, and, for the more adventurous, scuba dive from a number of small beaches, rocks, and coves.

One of the biggest attractions is the farm itself. Descriptive markers and photographs attached to the well-maintained historical buildings give details of the buildings' past lives. Visitors can explore the creamery, machine shop, barn, chicken coop, and house, which have all been preserved in their original settings. You can spend a pleasant and informative afternoon wandering around these buildings, learning how early settlers on Saltspring made a living.

Activities adjacent to the park

After visiting Ruckle, one of the most agreeable activities you can partake in is the exploration of Saltspring's quiet, twisting roads. This is ideal cycling country, especially in the spring and the fall or mid-week, when the island is less busy. Saltspring is renowned for its community of artists and craftspeople, many of whom open their roadside galleries and studios for passing travellers to visit, or who show their work at the Saturday market in Ganges' Centennial Park.

Ganges is the main centre of population on the island. It has a delightful two-kilometre seaside walkway to stroll along, boasts a number of coffee shops and cafes, and serves all commercial needs. Other activity sites on the island include a nine-hole golf course and Mount Maxwell Provincial

Park. From the top of Mount Maxwell you get a great view of other Gulf Islands. (This climb is not recommended for RVs.)

Summary

Ruckle is another excellent place to stay and enjoy British Columbia. The camping facilities overlooking Swanson Channel are superb and it is fun to watch the sun go down over the waters and see the BC Ferries light up as they travel between Vancouver Island and the mainland at night. Going to sleep here, with the waves lapping on the shoreline and the bright stars and moon casting shadows on the tent, is magical. When we stayed, a couple of seals who were just as interested in observing us as we were in them added to the enjoyment of sitting and watching the water. Those who choose to camp in an RV do not have immediate access to this vista, but it's only a short walk from the car park to the coast, where RVers can treat themselves to picnics by the water's edge.

Although the information boards in the park claim whales can be seen here, the BC Parks representative I spoke to stated that during the three years he had been at Ruckle he had not seen one. But you may be lucky. While we did not view them at Ruckle, we did see a whale on our return ferry ride to Vancouver. BC Ferries passengers often spot killer whales, and the ship's staff usually announces when they are in sight.

Salt Spring Island, A Place to Be from Heritage House is a treasury of information, stories, and pictures about this idyllic Gulf Island. Learn the history and secret gossip, and discover quaint accommodations.

Illustrated by local island artists, this is a keepsake for visitors and residents alike.

17. Fillongley Provincial Park

This provincial park on Denman Island, with its long sand-and-shingle beach, is a well-kept secret. While the crowds flock to Rathtrevor and Miracle Beaches during the peak summer months and camping spaces at these locations cannot be had for love nor money, little Fillongley with sands and shoreline comparable to its neighbours remains a tranquil haven.

My first visit was on a Sunday in July. We boarded the busy 2:00 p.m. ferry from Vancouver Island. It seemed every vehicle on the boat was equipped for camping, heading for Fillongley and *my* spot. As fate would have it, we were the third last car off the ferry, by which time most of our fellow passengers had sped away and we were left following a platoon of cyclists. We drove to Fillongley making alternative camping plans, but to our delight, upon arrival we found only three of the designated camping spots taken. Within a couple of minutes we were greeted by a large, grey-bearded man in vest, shorts, and earring, with a bicycle. He informed us he was the BC Parks officer. When questioned about his unconventional attire, he admitted he was not officially on duty and would return later to collect our fee. He also explained that while the marked camping spots offered little privacy, we could camp in the trees near the beach. He proceeded to lead us to what he deemed were the best spots. Very personal service for a $9.50 fee.

History

The park was bequeathed to the province by George Beadnell, who named it after his home in England. Beadnell was one of the first pioneers to come to the area. He built an estate that at its peak had a tennis court, bowling green, clubhouse, and greenhouse as well as a large impressive home. These facilities fell into disrepair and were vandalised following his death in 1958. They were eventually destroyed. Beadnell is buried in the park by the side of one of the trails (when I visited his grave there were fresh flowers on it). In 1978 the Comox *Free Press* reported on plans to expand the camping provision from 10 sites to 50, but when I was there this had not occurred.

Your own private spot in the trees near the beach.

You can camp out in the open at Fillongley or hidden in the trees.

Location

Denman Island, 19 kilometres long and 6 kilometres wide, is situated in the northern part of the Strait of Georgia between Vancouver Island and the mainland. The park, on the eastern side of the island, has stunning views of Lambert Channel. To reach Denman, take the hourly ferry service from Buckley Bay, which is 75 kilometres north of Nanaimo. The ferry ride is approximately 15 minutes and at the time of writing the round-trip cost for a vehicle with two passengers was $16.25. Upon reaching the island, follow the paved road four kilometres to the east coast and the campground. The 23-hectare provincial park contains a beach, a marshy estuary, a forest rich in old-growth firs, and the remnants of George Beadnell's estate.

Facilities

The biggest drawback at Fillongley is that there are only 10 gravel camping spots available and they are lined up side by side at the parking area with no vegetation around them, so they are anything but private. This is not too disastrous, as you can gain more privacy by pitching your tent either under nearby trees or, as we did, just a few feet from the beach and go to sleep with the sound of the waves lapping on the shoreline. All basic amenities are provided: wood (collected from the beach), water, pit toilets, picnic tables, fire pits. The park is wheelchair accessible; even the water pump has a ramp. I am in awe of anyone who can manipulate these pumps—some of them require a lot of strength—and doubly in awe of anyone who can do it from a wheelchair and collect water as it sporadically falls from this ancient device. The island has a restaurant, a couple of funky coffee bars, and stores that sell food, crafts, gas, and basic supplies.

Recreational activities

Hiking

Hiking trails through old-growth forest are an alternative to the shoreline recreational pursuits. These trails are not long. The Beadnell Trail leads past the namesake's grave and into a grassy meadow ringed by heritage trees with views of the sea. This walk can be completed in 20 minutes. The Creek Trail is about the same length and follows a stream to a salmon spawning ground. Interpretative boards detail this process.

Boating

The island, especially the beach at Fillongley, is a magnet for canoeists and kayakers. Kayaks can be rented from a shop in Denman Village.

Cycling

The island is ideal for cycling enthusiasts as there is little traffic (except near the ferry terminals) and it is relatively flat (except for one very steep hill when you leave the main centre of population). There are 48 kilometres of roads, about half of them paved. You can rent bikes from an outlet near the main concentration of shops. For those wanting a more rugged terrain, try Hornby Island (see below).

Fishing

Salmon fishing is reputed to be good from the southern end of the island, while two lakes, Chickadee and Graham, have trout fishing.

Family activities

The campground is situated near a lovely sand and pebble beach where it is possible to swim, beachcomb, and look for oysters and clams. Picnic tables have been placed close to the beach. Swimmers should be prepared for a long wade out if the tide is low, as the waters are shallow. Of course, this makes it safer for younger campers. When we visited, inventive dads were constructing rafts from driftwood.

Activities adjacent to the park

Denman Island is a delightful place to explore as it has a relaxed atmosphere and many craft and artist shops. At the southern tip of Denman is Boyle Point Provincial Park (no camping) with limited hiking trails and dramatic views of the ocean. In addition, Hornby Island, only a 15-minute ferry ride away, has hiking trails and lovely beaches. It has been termed the "undiscovered Hawaii of British Columbia." Hornby is hillier than Denman but has the same self-contained feel about it.

Summary

The Fillongley campsites are not as good as those at Miracle, Rathtrevor, or Long Beach, so if you want a spacious camping location with treed privacy you should choose these other sites. If, however, your primary desire is a quiet beach to wander along away from the crowds, then Fillongley fits the bill perfectly. This is not a location where the camper can expect to be entertained with a multitude of activities; it is a place to relax, unwind, and do nothing. One of my best camping memories is of finishing off a bottle of wine after dinner while sitting on the beach as the sun went down, watching two lonely kayakers paddle across the moonlit evening waters. We had spent the previous three nights camping at Stratchcona, where the mosquitoes were out in force, so it was delightful to relax in shorts and T-shirts in a haven without bugs.

Denman Island has experienced a leap in population growth in the last few years, a trend which is likely to continue, making me wonder whether this romantic little campground with its non-conformist BC Parks official will retain its charm into the twenty-first century.

18. Prior Centennial Provincial Park

To be truthful, this campground is not beautiful. It is relatively small, quite dark, close to a road, and on the flight path to an airport. However, it is the only provincial park campground on North or South Pender, so it grants economical access to these Gulf Islands that boast miles of magnificent shoreline and beaches, lovely wild flowers, open meadows, varied forests, abundant wildlife, and considerably less rain than Vancouver. Proof of the campground's extreme popularity can be found in the fact it accepts reservations for more than 75 percent of its available spaces, although in May and September the campground is rarely half full, even during weekends. Those wanting a "get-away-from-it-all" camping experience far from the rat race cannot go wrong in selecting Prior Centennial.

History

The Penders have seen a variety of developments since their early use, 6000 years ago, by the Coast Salish people (the Saanich and the Songhees), and the more recent visits by Spanish and British explorers of the eighteenth century. In the 1800s, small sheep farms were established by the early European settlers who started to farm and plant orchards, the remainders of which are seen all over the islands today. By the 1900s a government wharf, post office, and ferry service to Sidney on Vancouver Island signalled the presence of a vibrant community. The islands also experienced their fair share of logging in the 1940s and 1950s, a practice continued on a smaller scale into the 1980s. The provincial park was donated to BC Parks in 1958 by Mr. And Mrs. F.L. Prior, hence its name.

The Pender Islands, as well as all other islands in the Strait of Georgia, are protected under the Islands Trust, which was set up to preserve and protect the Gulf Islands and their unique amenities and environment for the benefit of those who live in the area and for the province as a whole. The Trust ensures land use and development in the area is handled with sensitivity, enabling the Gulf Islands to retain their charm.

Location

North and South Pender Islands lie just below the 49th parallel, midway between Vancouver and Victoria in the Strait of Georgia. Although linked by a one-lane wooden bridge, the islands retain very different characters— South Pender being quieter and less developed. About 3000 people live on the islands, with 2500 of them on North Pender. You can travel to the Penders via BC Ferries from Tsawwassen on the mainland (about two hours with stops at other Gulf Islands) or Swartz Bay on Vancouver Island (35 minutes non-stop or one to two hours with stops). The campground is located on North Pender, six kilometres from the ferry terminal on Canal Road.

Medicine Beach, a short walk from Prior Centennial.

Facilities

This is a relatively small, 16-hectare provincial park nestled in a pleasant wooded area. Seventeen well-spaced vehicle/tent sites are set in a densely forested area along a potholed circular road. Those with large RVs may have difficulty accessing some of these. All basic services can be found here (wood, water, fire pits, pit toilets, picnic tables). Reservations are accepted for all but five of the spaces. As mentioned above, the campground is close to the road, which is not busy at night, and seems to be under an airline flight path. The Driftwood Centre—with supermarket, liquor store, gift shop, bakery, gas station, bank, and deli—is two kilometres from the park. For those who don't want to cook on an open fire, the Inn on Pender Island has a restaurant and pizzeria and is conveniently located next door to the campground, while the marina at Browning Harbour has an excellent breakfast cafe—frequented by the boating fraternity, locals, and campers—a pub, and good views. Both the Inn and the marina also offer accommodation.

Recreational activities

Hiking

A one-kilometre trail leads from the campground. Named the Heart Trail, it takes explorers through the forest to Ketch Road and is easy to complete.

Mount Norman Regional Park on South Pender Island features over 100 hectares of varied forest. Those who are fit enough to endure the 30-minute (one way) climb are rewarded with spectacular views of the Gulf Islands and the Olympic Mountains in the United States. A well-designed boardwalk with bench seats leads to this vista. From Mount Norman

Regional Park you can hike into Beaumont Provincial Marine Park (no vehicle access). In addition to these trails, the country lanes of Pender are wonderful for strolls.

Boating
The waters around Pender are ideal for canoeing and kayaking. Two marinas are located on North Pender, one on South Pender. All have kayak and canoe rentals. In addition, kayaks and canoes can be launched from numerous other waterfront locations.

Cycling
Both North and South Pender are made for cycling. South Pender is quieter and my personal preference. Cyclists should be aware that the island roads are characterised by numerous dips and sharp curves. Bicycles can be rented from Otter Bay Marina and South Pender Marina.

Fishing
The three lakes on the islands contain fish but do not offer great fishing possibilities. Ocean fishing is the preferred option.

Wildlife observation
You can regularly see eagles, hawks, deer, otters, seals, and even pods of killer whales from and on the island. (There are no bears, cougars, or other dangerous animals here, so a restful night in the tent is guaranteed.)

Family activities
North and South Pender Islands and the campground itself are not particularly geared for young families unless they are keen on outdoor activities. The provincial park is located a few hundred metres from Medicine Beach on Bedwell Harbour, an ideal site for beachcombing and shoreline explorations. The waters are clear and good for swimming, although the beach is stony. The three local marinas all have outdoor swimming pools and access to ocean swimming.

Activities adjacent to the park
On Saturdays throughout the summer you can purchase local produce and crafts at a Farmers Market held at the Driftwood Centre. The small settlement of Hope Bay is a pleasant place to relax and watch the world go by. Check out the village's galleries and coffee shops. North Pender Island also has a nine-hole golf course and tennis courts.

The Penders are only a short ferry ride from Galiano and Saltspring Islands, which both have provincial parks, and from Mayne Island and Saturna with no provincial park camping. Many tourists vacation by "island hopping," while residents of the Lower Mainland and Vancouver Island visit to enjoy the altogether different ambience.

The view goes on forever at the summit of Mount Norman Regional Park.

Summary

Prior Centennial is not a picturesque campground, but it is conveniently located. I last stayed in late September when early sundown and cool evening temperatures necessitated a search for non-campground-based activities. I found them a two-kilometre walk away at the Browning Harbour Marina Pub, which has a pool table, darts, good food, and live entertainment on both Friday and Saturday nights. The venue was busy and very friendly as locals mixed with visitors. We viewed rainbows and sunsets through large picture windows that command hypnotic views of the harbour. The pub operates a designated driver system, so if you do consume too much alcohol, a free driver service is provided—just one more of many reasons to make the Pender Islands a stop on your camping itinerary.

Additional Recommendations

Smelt Bay (Map reference 34) You can reach this campground, on the southern peninsula of Cortes Island, by taking two ferries from Campbell River. It has only 22 places and all basic facilities (water, wood, pit toilets, picnic tables, and fire pits). The scenic island is ideal for canoeing and kayaking, while the campground has access to a long, pebbled beach.

Newcastle Island

THE BEST COASTAL MARINE PARK CAMPGROUNDS

Porteau Cove • Newcastle Island
Sidney Spit • Desolation Sound

British Columbia's first provincial marine park was Montague Harbour on Galiano Island (see Chapter 4). It was established in 1959 to give the boating public access to shoreline facilities amid some of the best waters in the world. The director of B.C.'s parks system defined a marine park as an area of scenic marine landscape with useable upland and sheltered foreshore on waterways designed to provide anchorages, moorings, resting places, campsites, and pleasurable places for boaters. More recently this definition has changed to emphasize outdoor recreation and conservation of the marine environment.

Rebecca Spit, Plumper Cove, Newcastle Island, and Sidney Spit were developed in 1960/61. By 1985 there were 28 marine parks. Ten years later there were 38 and the prognosis for further development is good.

Most marine parks have safe water anchorage and mooring buoys. Some have landing floats, quays, and campgrounds. Some are totally undeveloped. Consequently, the fees charged vary. BC Parks produces *Coastal Marine Parks of BC*, a leaflet including maps of these 38 parks.

A number of marine parks are not just the domain of boaters but are easily accessible to landlovers. In selecting these campgrounds, I wanted to show the variety of facilities accessible to people in southwestern B.C. **Porteau Cove** is a marine provincial park that can be reached by vehicle, with accommodation for the largest RV as well as moorings for the boating fraternity. **Newcastle Island** and **Sidney Spit** are both inaccessible by road, but have walk-in camping within easy reach of major centres of population (Nanaimo and Sidney) and, of course, moorings. To camp on either of these islands you can drive to a small passenger ferry, unload the family and camping equipment, cross to the island, and walk to the campground. On the other hand, **Desolation Sound**, B.C.'s largest provincial marine park, offers limitless wilderness camping experiences with few facilities and can only be reached by water.

19. Porteau Cove Provincial Marine Park

The word "Porteau" is taken from the French phrase *porte d'eau*, which means "water gate." Although essentially a marine park, Porteau Cove can be reached by water, road, and rail, so is open to all camping enthusiasts. Its stunning views of Howe Sound and its location, surrounded by the imposing elevations of the Coast Mountains, coupled with its easy accessibility from Vancouver, make it one of the most popular camping spots for boaters, RVers, and tenters in B.C.

History

The first European settlers to explore the area were the Spanish, who arrived in the late eighteenth century. Howe Sound was originally named Boca de Carmelo, but when British explorer Captain George Vancouver arrived, he renamed the waterway after his friend the Right Honourable Richard Scrope, Earl of Howe.

John F. Deeks named this area Porteau Cove when he opened a sand and gravel pit here in 1908 to serve the building industry in Vancouver. The community of Glen Eden, now no longer in existence, grew up around the industry and was serviced by steamships travelling up the fjord. In its heyday there were badminton and tennis courts here. The railway reached Porteau Cove in 1955, providing the first land link to Vancouver. It was followed ten years later by the highway. Porteau Cove became a marine park in 1981, and in 1996 a new railway station was built, suggesting the campground will remain accessible and popular.

Porteau Cove has stunning views of Howe Sound.

Location

Porteau Cove is located 12 nautical miles north of Horseshoe Bay in the most southerly fjord in North America: Howe Sound. The 50-hectare park can also be reached by road, 25 kilometres from Horseshoe Bay on the spectacular and aptly named Sea to Sky Highway, or by train from Vancouver and Whistler, so even if you do not own a vehicle or boat, you can still appreciate its splendour.

Facilities

The campground boasts 59 vehicle camping spots in addition to 15 walk-in sites. The walk-in sites are smaller and equipped with tent pads. They share a communal fire pit. All amenities, including showers, flush toilets, sani-station, disabled access, campground host, and reservations, make Porteau Cove probably the most developed marine park in the province. The best camping spaces are the reservable ones, with views of the sea and the mountains on Vancouver Island, and with access to a pebbled beach. While not as large as in other provincial parks, the spots offer privacy since they are surrounded by Sitka spruce trees. The campground is set away from the road, so traffic noise is not a problem, but the railway does run close by and there are a number of trains that pass during the day. You can buy food in Britannia Beach, eight kilometres north, while gas and other provisions are available farther north in the town of Squamish.

Recreational activities

Hiking

From the campground, a short trail up a wooden-stepped boardwalk leads west of the walk-in campsites to a view of the cove. Interpretative boards at the lookout describe the ecology and fauna and flora of the area. While there are no long hiking or walking excursions within the park, there are numerous trails and hikes just a short drive away, making this a good base for those who want to explore the Coast Mountains, Cypress Park (no camping facilities) to the south, and Garibaldi Provincial Park (which only has wilderness camping) to the north.

Boating

The public boat launch at Porteau Cove is the only one between Squamish and Horseshoe Bay, and numerous people take advantage of it. It is easy to launch canoes and kayaks from the beach to explore the nearby waters, and windsurfing is also possible here.

Diving

One of the biggest attractions at Porteau Cove is scuba diving. In 1981, when the park was opened, a ship was purposely sunk to form a reef.

Hiking at Porteau offers you an interpretative trail and lookout over the campsite and Howe Sound.

Today more vessels lie on the ocean floor to entice marine life and create a diving haven for enthusiasts. This also provides entertainment for the rest of us, as we can watch funny-looking rubber-clad individuals plunge into the cool waters. Interpretative boards on the beach describe the boats that lie on the ocean floor. The moderate water depths, gentle currents, and a specially-equipped change house make this one of *the* best diving locations in southwestern B.C. Divers can view red snapper, flounder, starfish, sea anemone, and octopus amongst the reefs. There are showers on the beach where divers can rinse off after emerging from the water.

Family activities

It is possible to swim and to snorkel in the waters of Howe Sound away from the diving area. A sand and gravel beach provides sunbathing opportunities, while a few lucky campers have direct access to the water's edge from their campsites. The park is an extremely popular picnic spot for people travelling along the highway.

Interpretative programs are offered Thursdays to Mondays during the summer. These take place in the amphitheatre and often include film and slide shows, talks, and Jerry Rangers activities for children. There are a number of interpretative boards in the park that describe the area and its inhabitants.

Activities adjacent to the park

The Mining Museum at Britannia Beach, a short drive north of the campground, is well worth a visit if you have time. You get to wear a hard hat as you take a tour that includes a rail trip underground and a demonstration of historic mining machinery including slushers, muckers, and drills. The museum, which houses an exhibition detailing the history of the mine, was recently declared a National Historical Site. There are also a number of arts and craft shops and cafes to visit in Britannia Beach.

Slightly farther north is Shannon Falls Provincial Park with spectacular views of the 335-metre falls (six times higher than Niagara). These falls are particularly dramatic in the spring and early summer, as the volume of water increases with the snow melt. In winter they freeze, forming stunning ice sculptures.

Summary

Porteau Cove is *very* busy, so expect to be disappointed if you plan to camp here during July and August without a reservation. If you are travelling the Sea to Sky Highway, it is a popular place to stop and enjoy breathtaking views across Howe Sound to Anvil Island in the southwest and the Tantalus range of mountains to the north. I first travelled this highway in 1985, during my first visit to B.C. It lived in my mind as one of the most beautiful roads in the world. Upon returning to the province in 1991, I was worried that time might have affected my perceptions and my memory could have embellished its splendour. I need not have been concerned. I have now travelled this route countless times and still regard it as the most beautiful in the world.

20. Newcastle Island Provincial Marine Park

In the summers of 1995, 1996, and 1997, the Campa Big Band played in the Newcastle Island pavilion. On each of these occasions my partner and I left our Vancouver home with rucksacks on our backs, caught two buses to the ferry at Horseshoe Bay ($1.50), took the ferry from Horseshoe Bay to Nanaimo ($8.00), and walked the 30-minute route from the ferry terminal to the quaint paddle steamer that takes us over to the Island. We hiked the trails during the day, ate on the veranda of the licensed tea rooms during the evening, then danced the night away to the sound of brilliant jazz music played by 18 top-quality performers. I think we were the only couple wearing shorts, but we had such fun for only $17.00 (price includes the dance and the steamer ride from Nanaimo, normally $4.00 return). It is delightful to round off a perfect day with a glass of whisky, music still ringing in your ears, and to know that your bed is just a short walk away across the starlit fields. Newcastle Island is a magical place and I am almost reluctant to tell others of its magic for fear that it will become too popular.

History

This 306-hectare marine park, encompassing an entire island, has a checkered and colourful history. It is named after England's famous coal-mining town. In 1853, with the help of the local native population, the Hudson's Bay Company established coal-mining operations on the island, the remains of which are still clearly visible today. Prior to this the Coast

Dance the night away to the sound of jazz on Newcastle Island.

*Newcastle Island is characterised by sandstone cliffs,
caves, tranquil coves, and gravel and sand beaches.*

Salish people inhabited the area. You can see evidence of their burial caves along the north and west shoreline.

Japanese Canadians operated a herring saltery and shipyard on the island from the early 1900s until 1941, when the Canadian government confiscated their property and sent them to internment camps in the Interior. Between 1941 and 1955, the Canadian Pacific Steamship Company used the island as a resort. The company built a dance pavilion, tea house, soccer pitch, and wading pool, and attracted as many as 1500 people a day during the resort's heyday. Photographs of this era are displayed in the pavilion. A sandstone quarry and a pulpstone quarry also operated on the island at different times during this century. In 1961, Newcastle Island was designated a provincial marine park.

Location

This provincial park is a small island barely a kilometre from Nanaimo, with spectacular views across the Strait of Georgia to the coastal mountains. The island is characterised by steep sandstone cliffs, caves, tranquil coves, and gravel and sand beaches. For those who do not have their own craft, a delightful little paddle steamer operates from Maffeo Sutton Park, behind the Civic Centre in Nanaimo, to ferry foot passengers to the island. Although this mode of transporting supplies to your campsite may put some off, many campers drive the family vehicle to the dock and unload tents, suitcases, rucksacks, coolers, bikes, dogs, and children in preparation for a weekend's stay on the island. The ferry staff is willing to accommodate all this equipment and there are carts available on the island

Newcastle's pavilion offers enchanting tea rooms and evening dancing.

that you can use to convey camping supplies from the dock to the camping areas.

Facilities

There are only 18 designated camping spots, positioned at the edge of the forest (many regularly visited by the island's rabbit population). A vast grassland meadow accommodates all additional campers. Many prefer this open space, which is closer to the water, over the designated spots. There are flush and pit toilets and the park is wheelchair accessible. BC Parks is upgrading the facilities and installed two showers in 1997—one in each washroom ($1.00 for a three-minute shower). Water, wood, fire pits, and picnic tables are provided, and there are large wooden boxes where you can store food that might otherwise be carried off by the island's raccoon population. Group camping is also available. Services are available in Nanaimo, although food can be purchased in the enchanting tea rooms located in the pavilion on the island. These are open from 7:00 a.m. until 7:00 p.m. during the summer.

Recreational activities

Hiking

One of the joys of Newcastle Island is the maze of hiking trails winding across and around the park. The popular Shoreline Trail takes about three hours to complete and follows the cliff edge to Nares Point on the northern side of the island. There is a vantage point where hikers can rest and watch the ferries arrive and depart (Giovando Lookout). This trail leads hikers to quieter areas of beach away from the main centre of activity and the marina at the island's southern end. Information boards along its length detail the island's mining history.

Other trails lead across the middle of the island to Mallard Lake and Kanaka Bay, where the body of a nineteenth-century murderer is buried in an unmarked grave. None of the trails are too arduous and all are well signposted.

Boating
As you would expect at a provincial marine park, there is lots of boat activity at Newcastle Island. There are berthing facilities for over 50 boats. The waters adjacent to the park are popular with kayakers and canoeists who explore the coves and beaches, many of which are only accessible from the water. Water-skiing is permitted in Nanaimo Harbour and Departure Bay, but not near the Newcastle Island ferry route. At low tide you can wade to neighbouring Protection Island, only a short distance away.

Cycling
Mountain bikes are permitted on two trails: the Kanaka Bay and Mallard Lake Trails. Both are easy to complete and while offering enjoyment to a family or recreational cyclist, do little to challenge the serious mountain bike enthusiast.

Fishing
The fishing here is not great, although it is possible to catch small fry from the wharf. A number of local marinas arrange boat rentals and fishing excursions for those who want to fish for salmon farther offshore.

Wildlife observation
In the evening you can see deer grazing in the open grassland area. The park also attracts an array of shore birds.

Family activities
There are sandy beaches and swimming at the area near the dock and at Kanaka Bay and Mark Bay. The vast expanse of grass, with numerous picnic tables, is an ideal location for picnicking and ballgames. There is an adventure playground, horseshoes, and a giant checkerboard, and during the summer months BC Parks offers walks, talks, and other activities focusing on the natural and human history of the area. Check the information boards at the pavilion or the dock for a list of the events.

Activities adjacent to the park
You can take the paddle steamer from Newcastle Island to visit the city of Nanaimo. Wander into town along the recently extended sea wall, "people watching" as you go. Coffee bars, restaurants, and gift shops start popping up the closer you get to downtown Nanaimo. Unfortunately, this sea wall does not yet extend as far as the Departure Bay ferry terminal.

The Centennial Museum in Piper Park has fascinating exhibits on the area's coal-mining past, which dates from 1853 to 1965. The museum also covers the time before European settlement, when the region was home to the Coast Salish people. Another museum is located in The Bastion, an octagonal edifice built by the Hudson's Bay Company in 1853 as a fort to protect miners.

Despite its rich and varied cultural history, Nanaimo may be best known for its bathtub race. Each July, vessels of various shapes and sizes attempt to navigate the Strait of Georgia en route to the finish line in Departure Bay (prior to 1997 the finish line was in Vancouver). Expect colour and excitement if you visit during this annual jamboree.

Summary

I had lived in Vancouver for three years before I learned of Newcastle Island. After visiting, I enthusiastically sang its praises to a number of friends. Many of them had lived in the Lower Mainland for years but had no knowledge of the place. It was as if BC Parks wanted to keep it a secret. While the camping facilities here will not appeal to those who depend on an RV or who demand access to a vehicle, for those with a boat or for people like me who want to sojourn at a tranquil location just a stone's throw from civilisation, Newcastle Island is perfect. You can also visit on a day trip for swimming and picnicking. This is one of my favourite B.C. parks.

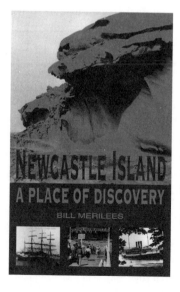

NEWCASTLE ISLAND
A PLACE OF DISCOVERY
BILL MERILEES

Look for the new book *Newcastle Island, A Place of Discovery* by Bill Merilees. The author's collection of historic photos includes many great portraits of Newcastle's heyday as well as historic maps. A must read for visitors to Newcastle Island.

21. Sidney Spit Provincial Marine Park

Sidney Spit Provincial Marine Park has a number of things to boast about: easy access from Vancouver Island; kilometres of sand and pebble beach; sheltered moorings; two long, sandy spits; shady, tree-lined walks; and a good selection of wildlife. BC Parks literature describes Sidney Spit as "one of the most beautiful marine parks in the Pacific Northwest," with thousands of metres of white sandy beach backed by towering bluffs. Beyond these the uplands contain a second-growth forest of fir, maple, western red cedar, and arbutus. One of the park's main features is a lagoon that offers an outstanding opportunity to explore intertidal life. These salt marshes and tidal flats attract both human and animal forms: ornithologists, naturalists, seals, orcas, and dolphins are all regularly seen.

The park is at the northern end of Sidney Island, which was formed thousands of years ago by glaciers that originated in the Cowichan Valley. As the glaciers retreated, they left behind islands of sand and gravel. More recently, the ocean currents have been eroding the island's southern end and depositing sand to form the spit, lagoon, and hook that can be seen today.

History

Hudson's Bay Company officers originally called this Sallas Island, but it was renamed Sidney by Captain George Richards, who undertook hydrographic surveys in the area during the mid-1800s. In 1902, George Courtenay of Victoria bought the entire island for $25,000. He farmed the land, cut the wood for railway ties, and established a brick factory in 1906. At its peak this factory employed 70 workers, mostly Chinese men, and produced 55,000 common and pressed bricks. Some of the bricks from this factory were used to build the famous Empress Hotel in Victoria and the Hotel Vancouver in Vancouver. The factory closed during the First World War. You can see evidence of this early history in the form of broken bricks scattered along the shoreline and the now grass-covered hills and hollows from which the clay was taken. A large meadow on the shore adjacent to the lagoon contains the remains of the Island Brick and Tile Limited mill.

In 1924, the Todd family began purchasing land on Sidney and by 1968 owned all but one tenth of the island. This 400 hectares was acquired by the government in 1924 and is the portion we all have access to today.

Location

This lovely camping facility has no vehicle access. There is sheltered anchorage on the west coast of the spit and there are a wharf and landing floats for small craft. If you do not have your own boat you can reach Sidney Island by taking a foot passenger ferry that departs hourly from

Whether you choose to camp out in the open or snuggle up to the trees, Sidney Spit campground is a 15-minute walk from the ferry.

the government wharf at the end of Beacon Avenue in Sidney. The 20-minute trip cost $7.00 return at the time of writing. The community of Sidney is just two nautical miles from the park across some very busy waters.

Facilities

The park has 20 formal camping spots about a 15-minute walk from the quay. There are also group camping facilities and plenty of space for overflow camping in a wide, grassy area, so everyone who visits is guaranteed a place to pitch a tent. All the basic amenities are provided (pit toilets, wood, water, fire pits, picnic tables). Services are found in Sidney. Be warned: although the water on the island is fit to drink, it tastes a little salty.

Recreational activities

Hiking

A number of short easy trails lead around the park (some of these are currently being upgraded). One of the longer ones (about six kilometres return) leads from the quay to the Marine Life Research Centre. This grand name conjures up images of a huge laboratory. In fact, it is a rather dilapidated hut—so dilapidated that the research scientists choose to camp outside. The trail is varied, with little elevation gain, and takes walkers along the seashore, through woodlands, and across meadows.

Fishing

Anglers can spin-cast for salmon at the end of the spit in the summer months, while Dungeness crabs are found in the eelgrass and waters of the lagoon.

Wildlife observation

The park is home to a variety of wildlife and it is not unusual to come across herds of over 20 black-tailed and fallow deer grazing in the island's meadows. In addition to the deer, rabbits, grouse, mink, river otter, tree frogs, blue herons, and eagles are also regularly seen. The large saltwater lagoon along the southwestern side of the park attracts many gulls, ducks, and geese and is alive with activity in the early hours of spring mornings. Over 150 species of birds visit the island. Interpretative boards in the park detail some of the island's wildlife.

Family activities

Sidney Spit is a real treat for young children, as it has thousands of metres of beach where they can play, fish, boat, beachcomb, sunbathe, and swim. The long teardrop shape of the spit ensures the beach never feels crowded. Once beach activities are over, the open grassy meadows are ideal for ballgames, while the numerous picnic tables provide shady locations for the consumption of food and drink. There are interpretative programs in July and August.

Activities adjacent to the park

The community of Sidney is a nice place for an afternoon stroll. A large proportion of the town's population is retired people and they seem to give Sidney a pleasant, relaxed ambience. There are shops selling arts, crafts, books (there are five bookstores in town), and antiques, in addition to inviting delis and cafes that offer an assortment of refreshments to revitalise a tired camper. Near the wharf, the Sidney Marine Mammal and Historical Museum displays pioneer and native artifacts in addition to exhibitions on the creatures that live in the adjacent waters (seals, sea lions, sea otters, and whales).

Summary

With almost 24 kilometres of shoreline, most of which is sand, it is easy to see why Sidney Spit attracts over 60,000 visitors a year. I last visited the park in early June 1997, when I expected the island to be quiet—an ideal time to undertake camping research. I boarded the private ferry from Sidney with just three other people: two women in their golden years and my partner. Before we reached the island, the noise hit us. A group of about 60 schoolchildren was on the quay, eagerly awaiting its return trip as two irate teachers tried to count the unruly mass to ensure none of their charges were being left on the island. (The teachers' red faces and hoarse voices confirmed this was a profession I did well not to pursue.) The captain of our small ferry looked with trepidation at his new passengers and explained to us that at this time of year the island was used for nature field trips by the local schools. He said he felt more like a schoolbus driver than the captain of a water taxi. Fortunately Sidney Spit is large enough to allow campers to avoid the chattering mass of enthusiastic young ones and their teachers. It's a perfect island for camping or to visit for the day.

22. Desolation Sound Provincial Marine Park

Located in what is reputed to be one of the finest cruising and kayaking regions in the world, Desolation Sound is the largest and most popular marine park in B.C. And for this reason alone has been included among the best marine parks. The 8000-hectare park includes over 60 kilometres of shoreline, several islands, a multitude of bays and coves, waterfalls, rivers, and freshwater lakes. Each summer, thousands of pleasure crafts leave their moorings in Washington State, the Lower Mainland, Vancouver Island, and farther afield to experience the splendid scenery and space offered in this park. It is not unusual for over 300 craft to be in the park during the summer months. Kayakers have also come to appreciate this intricate coastline. They leave their vehicles in one of two locations—the community of Lund, 23 kilometres north of Powell River, or Okeover Arm Provincial Park (with camping facilities), 10 kilometres south of Lund—and paddle in.

History

The first European travellers to the area included British and Spanish explorers who saw little value in the place. Captain George Vancouver wrote in his diary of 1792: "Our residence here is truly forlorn: an awful silence pervaded the gloomy forest, whilst animated nature seemed to have deserted the neighbouring country." Vancouver wrote in the late spring and as he regarded it as a remote, grim, unfriendly place, he gave it the name Desolation Sound.

It was viewed more positively in 1973, when the new provincial government decided to increase the number of parks in the province and established Desolation Sound Provincial Marine Park. Since then, BC Parks has tried to reduce the number of private holdings in the park. This policy has had some success, although there are still a number of privately owned properties. The park consists of 5600 hectares of upland and 2500 hectares of foreshore. In recent years, efforts have been made to build camping facilities, trails, and pit toilets.

Location

Desolation Sound Provincial Marine Park is on the northern shore of Gifford Peninsula, 32 kilometres north of Powell River. The nearest road access is nine kilometres away at the end of Highway 101 in Lund, where you can rent a canoe or kayak and set off to explore the park by yourself or sign up for an organised, group paddling excursion.

Facilities

Peter Chettleburgh in *An Explorer's Guide to the Marine Parks of BC* stated it is possible to cruise around Desolation Sound for two months and

Okeover Arm Provincial Park provides camping and a jumping-off spot for exploring Desolation Sound.

never anchor more than one night at the same spot. For kayakers or those who prefer not to sleep aboard their craft there are a number of wilderness camping facilities in the park. On-shore camping is permitted even where no facilities are provided, while you can find well-used wilderness spots at Lancelot Inlet, Grace Inlet, Galley Bay, Tenedos Bay, and Prideaux Haven. Some of these spots have pit toilets and fresh water, but campers must remember to carry fresh water, to pack out all garbage, and to check local regulations regarding fires. Prideaux Haven is thought to be one of the best boating destinations in the province, with numerous small islands, rocks, and an intricate shoreline providing some of the most exquisite coastal scenery and camping potential on the continent.

Recreational activities

It goes without saying that the main recreational activities here are boating, paddling, and sailing. The area has the warmest salt water in B.C. And consequently is an excellent place for swimming, diving, salmon fishing, and oyster catching (you will see a number of oyster farms in the vicinity). BC Parks literature describes the waters as "teeming with sealife."

For those who feel the need to stretch their legs, there are a couple of short trails. You can walk to Unwin Lake, a 173-hectare freshwater lake, by taking a well-travelled path from Tenedos Bay. You can fish for trout in the lake and, of course, swim. There is a small trail at Melanie Cove in Prideaux Haven. In addition, existing and abandoned logging operations have left roads to explore.

Summary

Some dedicated canoeists and kayakers contend that Desolation Sound is becoming too popular for their tastes, with encroaching powerboats

Okeover Inlet provides services for the boating crowd.

spoiling their enjoyment. Others believe it is the jewel in the marine park crown, with space for every type of water vessel, and they provide photographs and descriptions of the multitude of paddling and camping opportunities that exist in this watery wonderland. If you intend to explore B.C.'s largest marine park, consider reading Bill Wolferstan's *Cruising Guide to B.C. Volume II: Desolation Sound and the Discovery Islands*.

I have not kayaked or travelled to this park. For the most part, the people I spoke to who had camped in the region were enthusiastic about everything the park offers. There was only one notable cause for concern: they informed me the mosquitoes in these parts can be the size of bears.

Additional Recommendations

Montague Harbour See Chapter 4.

Beaumont Marine Park (Map reference 35) On the far west side of South Pender Island, this park is only accessible by boat. There are 11 camping spots and activities include beachcombing, walking trails, swimming, and fishing.

Portland Island/ Princess Margaret Marine Park (Map reference 36) This marine park became accessible to those without a craft in 1997, when water taxis started regular runs from Sidney to Portland Island, which has trails and swimming, fishing, and diving opportunities. Twenty camping spaces.

Smuggler Cove Marine Park (Map reference 37) This small park on the Sechelt Peninsula can be accessed by both road and sea. There are only five camping spots a 15-minute walk from the parking lot. There are short trails as well as fishing and swimming opportunities.

Saltery Bay

THE BEST CAMPGROUNDS TO KISS

Birkenhead Lake • Nairn Falls
Emory Creek • Saltery Bay

Plagiarism is the order of the day here, as the title of this chapter has been taken from the popular series of books *The Best Places to Kiss*. The series covers various areas besides the Pacific Northwest. While many unromantic non-campers find the thought of cuddling at a campsite implausible ("Who wants to kiss someone who has not washed for days?"), some of us know there is nothing more idyllic than kissing as nearby waves break on the shore of a deserted beach, or kissing to the sound of turbulent waters plunging over rock faces formed centuries ago, or simply kissing by the campfire embers under a star-filled sky.

Kissing, much like camping, is an activity of personal taste. Some abstain; others do it whenever they have the chance. Personal preference also determines the ideal camping environment for kissing. What appeals to one kisser will not to another, and there is no guarantee the reluctant kisser will be stirred to passion in the campgrounds I recommend.

These four campgrounds present a variety of places to kiss: waterfalls, rivers, lakes, and ocean. It naturally follows that these environments induce different types of kissing. The turbulent cascading waters at **Nairn Falls** spur long, passionate kisses; the ever-changing white waters of the Fraser River at **Emory Creek** inspire tender embraces; the tranquil lake at **Birkenhead** fosters prolonged smooches; the constant lapping of the clear salt waters of **Saltery Bay** may promote numerous gentle pecks. (As you can see, I have carried out extensive research.)

These campgrounds are not the most popular in the province. They offer few recreational activities, do not have showers, have no interpretative programs, and with the exception of Saltery Bay, do not accept reservations. They *do* provide "adult" camping experiences. While families will have fun (especially at Birkenhead and Saltery Bay where there is access to water), these campgrounds appeal more to couples or retired campers happy to pass time reading and relaxing away from crowds. Consequently, they are perfect places to kiss.

23. Birkenhead Lake Provincial Park

I knew I had to include Birkenhead Lake in a book on the best campgrounds—but where? Although it has a fabulous beach, the waters of the lake can be extremely cold, so it did not fit in the beach section of the text. There are wilderness hiking possibilities in the region, but few are directly accessible from the park. And although children can have a ball relaxing and playing in this environment, there is no formal program for kids. Birkenhead is not a marine park or an island park or a forestry campground, but it is such a perfect place to camp that it justified inclusion.

When I considered my affection for the place, I realised it was inspired by the park's location—on a lake surrounded by snowcapped mountains—and by the knowledge that I can leave Vancouver at midday on a Friday and be setting up tent at Birkenhead by 4:00 p.m. with a lovely relaxing weekend ahead. It is a little-known campground that always accommodates, and I recommend it as one of the best campgrounds to kiss because it is a quiet, away-from-it-all place. At dusk, nothing can beat a barbecue or a walk on the beach to the sound of the water gently lapping on the sands. Watch the sunlight fading as the ospreys soar overhead or dive into the water for fish. Stay as the moon appears and the stars come out in a sky far larger than the one that covers Vancouver. Appreciate the romance Birkenhead inspires as night arrives, then head back to your tent for...who knows?

History

The road to Birkenhead passes through the community of Mount Currie, home to the Lil'wat people for centuries. In the 1850s the road from Mount Currie to D'Arcy was part of the Douglas Trail, and fortune-seeking miners passed through these towns as they travelled north from Fort Langley to Lillooet en route to the gold of the Cariboo. The trail was abandoned in 1864 when the Fraser Canyon route opened. The town of D'Arcy, at the southern end of Anderson Lake, was a trading post of the Hudson's Bay Company during this time and was known as Port Anderson.

Location

Six kilometres long, Birkenhead Lake is surrounded by snowcapped Coast Mountains and blessed with clear waters. One of the best things about deciding to camp at Birkenhead Lake is the journey there. From Vancouver, the three-and-a-half-hour drive takes you on the fabulous Sea to Sky Highway along the fjord of Howe Sound, through Garibaldi Park, past the Whistler ski resort, and on to Pemberton. From Pemberton, continue to Mount Currie and then take the quiet, paved road through the mountains to D'Arcy. Just before D'Arcy, turn off onto a good, gravel road that takes you another 17 kilometres to the park. You can break your journey at Squamish, Whistler, Pemberton, Mount Currie, or at the other provincial parks on this road (Shannon Falls, Nairn Falls, Brandywine Falls, and Porteau Cove).

Facilities

There are 85 camping spaces available here, all but a few located in a beautiful deciduous forest with streams running beside them. These streams will keep your drinks cool on a hot summer day. There is a sani-station but no flush toilets. The park is not wheelchair accessible. The only other disadvantage is that some camping spots are near stagnant water pools, so mosquitoes can be a problem at certain times of the year. A few camping spaces are lined up away from the main site in a regimented manner. If the campground is full, there is a small BC Forestry Service campground on the gravel road leading to the campground. If you need supplies, there is a store in D'Arcy and gas stations and restaurants at Mount Currie.

Recreational activities

Hiking

A trail leads along one side of the lake and is used by mountain bikers and walkers. It takes about two hours to walk to the other end of the lake (four hours return) and is an easy hike. Watch out for bears and deer.

Boating

The lake is an ideal place to canoe or kayak, and although much of the dense forest reaches to the shores, there are a few private coves for sunbathing. There is a concrete boat launch for those who have their own craft, and when I last visited, BC Parks staff offered canoe rentals. There is a private development at the opposite end of the lake and the residents are not keen on having campers from the provincial park exploring "their" land. Thank goodness we have BC Parks to ensure that access to some of the best scenery in the world is not the privilege of a few.

Fishing

Fishing for kokanee, whitefish, rainbow trout, and Dolly Varden is reputed to be good, and both anglers and ospreys can be seen fishing here.

Wildlife observation

Watch for moose, black bear, mountain goats, and deer. You can often see ospreys and bald eagles circling over the waters of the lake, especially during the evening hours or first thing in the morning. Interpretative boards at the park detail the birds of the area.

Family activities

Birkenhead Lake has a lovely beach and protected swimming area, although the waters can be daunting as they come directly from the surrounding

Birkenhead, a perfect place to camp, is surrounded by mountains.
(courtesy BC Parks)

mountains' snow. The frigid temperature does not seem to bother children. The beach may be smaller early in the season if the waters are high, but in August and September this is not a problem. There are numerous picnic tables on a large grassed area by the lake. The gravel roads that ribbon through the campground are a safe cycling haven for young children, and youngsters can also have fun building dams and playing in the streams.

Activities adjacent to the park

There is not much additional activity in the vicinity of the park. The community of D'Arcy has a railway station and fantastic views of Anderson Lake, but little else.

Summary

The tranquil location coupled with the spectacular landscape and the pleasant drive from the Lower Mainland make Birkenhead Lake a delightful romantic spot to spend a weekend or longer. A few years ago my partner and I visited Birkenhead for the first time. We hiked the trail on a hot summer day and decided on a swim to cool off. We found a track leading to the water's edge, where a little beach seemed perfect for sunbathing after the swim. We didn't have any swimming gear with us, but since no boats were in sight we prepared for a skinny dip in the crystal clear waters of the lake. What could be more romantic? As mentioned, the waters of the lake can be very cold, so getting in was a slow event. Just as I was about to submerge my whole body, we heard a motorboat approaching. We ran back to the shore with this craft in close pursuit. I presumed the three men in the boat would diplomatically pull into another cove as I raced to put on my shirt and drape shorts in front of my bottom half (there was no time to put them on properly). Instead, the boat and its three occupants pulled into our cove. It was then I noticed these were not three ordinary men...these were two RCMP members and a BC Parks officer. Expecting to be ticketed for indecent exposure, for committing a vulgar and offensive act in public, or for polluting the water with a sweaty body (we were unsure whether skinny dipping was in the Canadian Criminal Code), I made jokes about looking after their boat as they politely passed the time of day and disappeared up the trail, making no comment on our activity or state of undress. The moral of this story? Never believe you are in the middle of nowhere when considering a romantic skinny dip (or any other deviant activity) with the one you love, as the Mounties will always be close at hand—like your mother was in days gone by—to ensure decorum is maintained.

24. Nairn Falls Provincial Park

Like the other campgrounds detailed in this section, what this location lacks in organised recreational activities it makes up for in peacefulness. Nairn Falls is not a campground for kids. I associate it with the older RVing crowd, retired people who have time on their hands and a desire to be amongst some of the best scenery in the world. These people do not need beaches, lakes, adventure playgrounds, interpretative programs, and visitors centres. They just want to be outdoors together to read and relax and reflect upon life. Nairn Falls is ideal for this.

The best place to kiss in this provincial park is at the falls themselves, but timing is all-important. Do not attempt a romantic excursion with the person of your dreams during the daytime, when all the daytrippers are out in force. If you do, your kiss will undoubtedly be disturbed as mothers yell to adventurous children not to get too close to the waters and 40 tourists, recently disembarked from their tour bus, try to wind their way around your embrace and take pictures. Wait until after dinner (remember a flashlight) and take the 20- or 30-minute stroll along the deserted trail from your campsite to the falls as the long evening shadows appear. Most other campers will have made this excursion during the day, so there is a good chance the falls will be all yours. Choose your position and kiss passionately to the sound of the Green River as it crashes over the rock face and plummets to the deep pools below.

History

Travelling to Nairn Falls involves taking Highway 99, named by some the "cliff-hanging highway." It passes through a dramatic landscape created thousands of years ago during the last ice age, when the coastal region sank under the immense weight of a glacier. Eleven thousand years ago, as the ice began to melt, the ocean rose and flooded inland, creating fjords such as Howe Sound, which Highway 99 follows from Vancouver to Squamish. The glacial action and the subsequent geographic and climatic conditions created three distinctly different waterfalls along the route: Shannon Falls, just south of Squamish and Canada's third highest waterfall (335 metres); Brandywine Falls, between Squamish and Whistler, with its unique horseshoe shape; and Nairn Falls. All three of these waterfalls are in provincial parks, with Nairn Falls Park created in 1966.

Location

Set in the majestic Coast Mountains just north of Garibaldi Provincial Park, this 171-hectare provincial park is 3 kilometres south of Pemberton, 29 kilometres north of Whistler on Highway 99. Its perch high on the banks of the Green River ensures the sound of rushing water is ever present. The falls themselves are away from the campground and plummet over a series of smooth rock faces into deep plunge pools. The park is extremely popular with picnickers and as a rest stop. Do not be put off if the day-use car lot is crowded; the campground is considerably quieter.

Facilities

I stayed here in July one year when the temperature was in the high 20s Celsius and really appreciated the shady canopy at this heavily wooded campground. It has 88 spacious camping spots in a forest of Douglas fir, cedar, and hemlock. Some overlook the canyon and all accommodate the largest RVs and give total privacy. Facilities include wood, water, fire pits, picnic tables, pit toilets, and a sani-station. Services are conveniently located in Pemberton or Whistler. At $9.50 per night the campground must provide the cheapest night's accommodation within a 30-kilometre radius of Whistler, where it is easy to spend $300 a night for a hotel room.

Recreational activities

Hiking

One easy-to-complete, well-maintained, 30-minute trail leads from the day-use area along Green River to the falls. It is exciting to hear the sound of the rushing water intensify as you reach the falls themselves, which plunge 60 metres over smooth rock before proceeding to Lillooet Lake. Other trails exist in the park, but when I visited they were badly signposted, making exploration difficult. Some of the lower trails along the river had been washed out.

The campground is a base from which to check out the hiking possibilities in 194,000-hectare Garibaldi Park (see the entry on Alice Lake in Chapter 2).

Fishing

Anglers can use spinners or flies to catch large rainbow trout and Dolly Varden in Green River. The challenge is getting close to the river. Green Lake, beside Highway 99, contains rainbows up to one kilogram, Dollies over three kilograms, and kokanee.

Family activities

There is not a lot for kids to do in this park, but a two-kilometre drive north will bring you to Pemberton Park, a great place for family fun. This lakeside park, to your right just before you enter Pemberton, is maintained by the municipality and has a grassy area for sunbathing, a small beach, a trail skirting its perimeter, and swimming. An added bonus is that the waters here are warmer than in many other lakes in the region.

Activities adjacent to the park

The rapidly changing town of Whistler, world-renowned as a ski resort, provides a multitude of things to see and do, from coffee shops and restaurants to gondola rides up the mountains, heli-skiing on glaciers, white-water rafting trips up the Green River, windsurfing, shopping, hiking, and golf. A pleasant urban trail winds through the community. My favourite activity in Whistler is undoubtedly people watching, as all nationalities are represented and everyone seems to be wandering around in a slow, relaxed, "don't-know-where-I'm-going" vacation haze. Choose a cafe in the central square and spend hours watching the diversity of people and street performers.

Summary

The shady peaceful campground at Nairn Falls offers a sophisticated, adult camping experience for those who want to escape from life's pressures. When I stayed here, the quiet was infrequently disturbed by the noise of powerboats ascending the rapids, taking groups of visitors through the white water. Excursions of this nature can be organised in Pemberton and Whistler and fortunately end around 5:00 p.m., returning the peace. Nairn Falls is an ideal location from which to explore Whistler (and is considerably cheaper than staying in the town). For those who are tired of smelling of woodsmoke and cooking over an open fire, romantic candlelit dinners are close at hand, with a choice of international cuisine only 30 minutes from the campground. The lack of recreational pursuits may put some people off, but for those who just want to be in the company of the one they love, Nairn Falls is a haven.

25. Emory Creek Provincial Park

A few years ago an advertising campaign for a large jewellery store had the slogan "Gold is for Lovers." Emory Creek, with its gold-mining history and gold-prospecting potential, is therefore a natural inclusion as one of the best campgrounds to kiss. When I purchase my first RV (I currently camp in a tent), it is my ambition to head to Emory Creek for at least three days, read books on the history of the 1860s gold rush, pan for gold, and (hopefully) kiss and be kissed on the banks of the famous Fraser River. Although I know as much about gold panning as I do about fishing, both activities appear to provide a wonderful excuse to sit for long periods of time at the water's edge with the illusion of being gainfully employed.

When BC Parks started the reservation system in 1996, Emory Creek was one of only two campgrounds removed from the process after a four-month trial period. The reason was that not enough campers were choosing this destination. This should not be discouraging. Like the other campgrounds detailed in this chapter, Emory Creek is an adult campground. Although frequently used as an overnight stop for those heading up the Fraser Canyon, it is also a lovely place to spend time, to unwind and relax with easy access to the waters of the Fraser. One of the best places to kiss is undoubtedly on the pebbly shore of the mighty river. Imagine the mountain-surrounded sky above, the sound of the waters rushing towards the Pacific, the smell of the barbecue as the fresh salmon caught only an hour previously cooks over the coals, and the sight of the well-used gold pan, empty but for the huge gold nugget that your loved one pulled from the waters earlier that day.

While you may not manage the salmon or the gold nugget, I promise the scenery and shoreline will furnish a fantastic romantic environment in which to kiss.

History

The first inhabitants of the area were the Sto:lo or Halq'emeylem people who lived by the river and farmed the oil-rich salmon. In 1808, Simon Fraser travelled the length of the river that now bears his name. He was an agent of the Northwest Company and a fur trader seeking passage to the Pacific. By the mid-nineteenth century the Hudson's Bay Company, which had taken over the Northwest Company, had established a number of forts and trading posts along the river and sent the locally discovered gold to San Francisco. It is hard to believe that the site of the campground was once Emory City, which at one time boasted 13 streets and a population of over 500 pioneers and gold-seekers. Emory City might still have existed today if the Canadian Pacific Railway had chosen it instead of Yale as its major centre. Instead, by the end of the nineteenth century the town was deserted and now nothing remains except its history. In 1956 the provincial government established a park at the site.

Location

This 15-hectare provincial park is conveniently located on Highway 1, the Trans-Canada Highway, 18 kilometres north of Hope, 6 kilometres south of Yale, on the banks of the majestic Fraser River. Further north, two of Canada's most famous rivers, the Thompson and the Fraser, converge. Consequently, the volume of water in the river as it passes the campground is considerable, especially during the winter and spring when it is a truly unforgettable sight.

Facilities

Nestled in a mixed forest area, the 34 large, private camping spots are suitable for every type of recreational vehicle. Some of the best sites offer views (and the rushing sound) of the water. One of the most distinctive features of this campground is the "flushing thunderboxes"— toilets that look like pit toilets from the outside, but which flush. On the two separate occasions I stayed in this park, these facilities not only flushed but also contained small holders with dried flowers and air fresheners. There is no sani-station nor showers nor disabled access. The transcontinental railway is adjacent to the park and the sound of trains, while audible, can be quite soothing (although there is a lot of traffic on this route). The town of Hope has all services, and there are a number of gas stations and cafes on the highway.

Recreational activities

Hiking

There is one small hiking trail leading from the park.

Fishing

Fishing is a popular recreational pursuit here, with salmon being the prime target. When I last stayed I spent an evening watching First Nations anglers stretch nets across the waters to catch the salmon.

Family activities

There is not a lot to do at Emory Creek, so the park seems to attract retired folk looking for a tranquil spot to spend a few days. During my last visit, two grey-haired gentlemen were busy panning for gold, which struck me as a pleasant and potentially profitable way to spend an afternoon. Gold pans can be purchased in Hope.

Activities adjacent to the park

The town of Yale, founded in 1848, was originally a Hudson's Bay trading post and is home to one of B.C.'s oldest churches, the Church of Saint

John the Divine, built in 1862 in the midst of the gold rush. Near the church is a museum detailing the town's past.

As you travel the Trans-Canada Highway's "Gold Rush Trail," you will see a number of interpretative boards that describe the history of the area. One of the most popular sights is Hells Gate, a 30-minute drive north of Emory Creek. Here the Fraser Canyon is at its narrowest, 30 metres wide, with water rushing through a gorge 180 metres deep. The Hells Gate Airtram takes visitors down for a close examination of the waters thundering through the canyon. Although it's a little commercialised, it is worth a visit. Also worth seeing are the Kettle Valley railway tunnels at Coquihalla Canyon Recreational Area just north of Hope (signposted from the Coquihalla Highway).

Summary

Simon Fraser wrote in 1808 that he had never seen anything like the Fraser Canyon, adding that his party had to pass "where no human should venture." Fortunately access today is easier, but the rugged mountains remain the same. This campground has a wonderful feeling about it. Its lack of structured activities makes it particularly appealing to older campers, while the well-cared-for and unique washroom facilities are a welcome surprise to seasoned campers who often approach pit toilets (especially in the height of summer) with deep dread. Emory Creek does not appeal to everyone. It is not large, nor does it boast a hundred and one activities, and it *is* close to the road and railway line. However, it is also quaint, unrushed, and a unique camping location ideal for kissing.

26. Saltery Bay Provincial Park

Have you ever sat in the dentist's waiting room reading *National Geographic*, looked at those atmospheric photographs, and wondered, "Do such beautiful places actually exist?" They do, and Saltery Bay is one of them. A feature on Saltery Bay in the prestigious *National Geographic* is testimony to its unique beauty. This is a relatively small, quiet campground, and its real draw is the superb scenery of Jervis Inlet. I have selected it as a romantic campground because of this vista.

"Do such beautiful places actually exist?" They do, and Saltery Bay is one of them.

Again, dusk is when the romantic ambience is best appreciated. A couple of picnic tables have been placed on the rocks adjacent to the waters, so it is possible to have a moon-lit dinner while listening to the waters lapping on the smooth rocks. In the early evening, bats circle overhead while seals swim in the waters and otters play on the rocks. Stay at this waterfront location as the sky reddens, then darkens to reveal a view of the galaxy that often includes shooting stars. This environment moves even the most unromantic and is highly conducive to kissing.

History

Saltery Bay is named for a fish saltery that was located here at the turn of the century. The Sliammon people have lived in the area for over 2000 years and you can see evidence of their long-term presence today in the mounds of seashells on the beaches near the campground. The first European to visit the area was Captain Vancouver in the late seventeenth century. Logging, which remains the backbone of the economy, started in the eighteenth century and received its biggest impetus at the turn of the century when the Powell River Paper Company (which later merged with MacMillan Bloedel) set up a pulp and paper mill in Powell River in 1910. The area's economy is still dependent on the mill, which continues to employ over 1000 people, although the area is also becoming known for tourism.

Location

Visitors travelling from Vancouver must take the ferry from Horseshoe Bay to Langdale (45 minutes), then travel Highway 101 to Earls Cove (90 minutes) and catch a second ferry to Saltery Bay (50 minutes). Saltery Bay Provincial Park is one kilometre from the ferry terminal, on the north shore of Jervis Inlet. The enchanting land and sea route from the Lower Mainland, and the ocean view at Saltery Bay make this camping excursion a real delight. From Vancouver Island, you can take the ferry from Comox to Powell River (about 75 minutes) and then drive 27 kilometres south of Powell River to the park.

Facilities

This campground is a perfect size with 42 large, private sites in an evergreen forest. Good gravel roads accommodate all types of recreational vehicles. Desirable spots are close to a creek that babbles constantly amongst the mature trees and rich vegetation. The campground has a sani-station but only pit toilets and no showers. It is wheelchair accessible and accepts reservations. A day-use area is two kilometres north of the campground. All services are in Powell River.

Recreational activities

Hiking

The Mermaid Trail winds through the park and takes about 15 minutes to complete. There is also a walk by the water's edge that leads to the rocks by the sea. As the area is dominated by logging, there are a number of rough roads and trails to explore, and the township of Powell River has actively developed additional trails (see "Activities adjacent to the campground").

Boating

There is a boat launch at the day-use area of the park, and the waters of Jervis Inlet offer canoeing and kayaking possibilities. These opportunities extend beyond the immediate area of the park (see Desolation Sound in Chapter 5) and include the Powell Forest Canoe Route, where you can spend a week canoeing a series of lakes.

Diving

In addition to the scenery, the biggest attraction here is the shallow offshore waters of the park. Scuba divers are enticed to the area by the variety of marine life, underwater cover, and shipwrecks to explore. There is also access for disabled divers. A three-metre-long bronze mermaid has been placed underwater at Mermaid Cove in the park, to the delight

Don't forget your fishing rod when you visit Saltery Bay.

of many divers. This mermaid has the honour of being Canada's first underwater statue. A number of other diving sites can be found in the 50-kilometre stretch of water between Lund and Saltery Bay.

Fishing

From the rocks at Mermaid Cove you can fish for salmon in the waters of Jervis Inlet. The numerous lakes and rivers in the area also have good fishing potential.

Wildlife observation

You may see killer whales, seals, and sea lions, which occasionally bask in the area, in addition to sea otters, bats, and bald eagles.

Family activities

This campground is not specifically oriented for families, although the nearby beach areas do offer entertainment for children.

Activities adjacent to the campground

The community of Powell River, a scenic 30-minute drive north, is worth a visit. Diners can choose from a number of little cafes and restaurants (try the Java Jungle with an animal theme—even the women's toilet is painted like a zebra. More importantly, the food is good).

Visitors can take a walking tour of the historic town, including the Pacific Theatre, the oldest operating movie theatre in B.C. It still has organ music prior to the film presentation. Staff at the Visitors Centre can give you details of the area's many attractions, which include a 13-kilometre, wheelchair-accessible trail around Inland Lake (see Chapter 7). The town is currently developing a 183-kilometre trail that will stretch from the end of Malaspina Peninsula to Saltery Bay. This will rival the famous West Coast Trail. If you have time, make an excursion north of Powell River to the community of Lund, known for its abundant supply of fish, clams, crabs, and oysters.

Summary

When I was researching this book, I had planned to spend just one night at Saltery Bay before heading over to Vancouver Island. I ended up staying four nights over the Labour Day weekend. The weather was good and the campground never full. The pleasure of staying at this campground comes not only from the clear salt waters for which it is known, but also from the north Sunshine Coast environment. The community of Powell River is a caring community. It had the first medical plan in B.C., the first credit union, and today is a town making concerted efforts to accommodate people with disabilities, as can be seen by the brilliant facilities for wheelchairs provided at Saltery Bay and other local parks (see the Inland Lake entry in Chapter 7). It is a town you want to spend time in.

The four nights I spent at Saltery Bay all included dinner by the campfire followed by a walk to Mermaid Cove to watch the sun go down. On our last night, any ambitions I had to create a romantic scene were shattered. Four divers with bright lights had chosen this time to view herring, crabs, starfish, and, of course, the bronze mermaid. Their observations were loudly relayed to their colleagues and me. Romantic excursions may have to be put on hold if the divers are out.

Additional Recommendations

Campfires Gazing into the campfire as the night draws in and the stars come out is a cliché, but in my experience a campfire produces an environment conducive to kissing (as long as it is not raining). Therefore all campgrounds, no matter where they are, can inspire romance provided you choose the right person to camp with—and there is not a ban on campfires.

The Best Beach Campgrounds All the campgrounds detailed in Chapter 3 are suitable for romance provided the crowds have gone and the beach is yours. Pacific Rim may be the best bet as it is considerably larger than the others and therefore offers the potential for solitude.

The Best Island Campgrounds Islands are wonderful places for love. The campgrounds recommended in Chapter 4 promote affection.

Inland Lake

7

THE BEST FREE CAMPGROUNDS

Chilliwack Lake/Chilliwack River
Chehalis Lake/Chehalis River
Inland Lake • Weaver Lake

While the cost of camping is not considerable compared to many other activities (at time of writing, provincial parks charged a maximum of $15.50, while private campground fees were as high as $30.00 a night), the notion of camping for free is a popular one, for obvious reasons. Although the uninhabited areas of the province offer limitless possibilities for free camping, the BC Forestry Service (BCFS) maintains a number of sites specifically designated for camping for which no fee is charged. Most of these are in remote, scenic areas far from main roads and centres of population, therefore providing a real wilderness camping adventure.

Anyone accustomed to camping in private or provincial park campgrounds where fresh water, firewood, and regularly cleaned toilets (with copious quantities of toilet paper) are all taken for granted, should be prepared for a new experience when staying at a BCFS site. One of the biggest differences is often the campground's location. Many are at the end of 30 kilometres or more of twisting, rough, logging road that is unsuitable for large RVs, trailers, cars, or anything other than a 4x4 or truck. The scenery these roads traverse and the access they grant to the B.C. wilderness are exceptional, but you must give serious consideration to the wear and tear on your vehicle, not to mention on you and the rest of your crew. For many, the expenditure saved does not justify the possible damage to the camping vehicle.

The camping facilities and services offered vary from site to site but generally are much more rudimentary than those in provincial parks. There is usually at least one toilet (with or without paper and with a door that might stop a foot above the ground), wooden or concrete picnic tables,

BCFS are user maintained campsites.

and water—though it frequently has to be taken from a river or stream. The camping spots are not carefully set up, so people accustomed to camping in provincial parks might find them primitive and even scruffy. Some campsites have fire pits or a fire ring, firewood, and garbage cans; others do not. With a few exceptions, BCFS sites are user maintained, so they might feature burnt garbage in the fire pit or elsewhere, courtesy those unscrupulous users who have not followed the "pack out what you pack in" rule. The campgrounds tend to be small; it is quite unusual to find a BCFS site accommodating more than 20 vehicles, although there are some that house more and are almost of provincial park quality (see Inland Lake, Tamihi Creek, and Chehalis River below). Most are located near a river, stream, or lake and afford outdoor enthusiasts the chance to sleep amongst some of the most breathtaking scenery in the world. These sites are for campers who want an isolated wilderness experience, not developed facilities.

The following pages describe some of the best free camping opportunities in the Lower Mainland. The first area features eight campgrounds along a 50-kilometre stretch of road running beside the **Chilliwack River and Chilliwack Lake**. This is probably the best concentration of BCFS campgrounds in the Lower Mainland and gives both the RV camper and tenter a number of alternatives. There are also a number of recreational opportunities available that require minimal driving on rough roads, another justification for their inclusion. In contrast, three of the four camping facilities detailed at **Chehalis Lake/Chehalis River** are more remote and promise those who can access them a true wilderness camping experience. **Inland Lake** is not only a fantastic BCFS site, but also offers excellent camping facilities for the disabled, rivaling many provincial parks. Finally, the campground at **Weaver Lake** is small and serene and I chose it as a typical example of the provision offered by BCFS. In total, I describe 14 free campgrounds in southwestern B.C.

This chapter could easily have been titled "Best Fishing Campgrounds in Southwestern B.C.," as there are fishing opportunities at Chehalis Lake/Chehalis River and Chilliwack Lake/Chilliwack River. Indeed, many of the regular users of BCFS campgrounds, especially in the quieter seasons, are anglers who are not at all bothered by the quality of the campground as long as the nearby waters are accommodating.

27. Chilliwack Lake/Chilliwack River, BCFS

The eight camping sites in this area make up the best concentration of free campgrounds in the region. All are located near or on Chilliwack Lake or Chilliwack River, scattered along Chilliwack Lake Road, requiring minimal driving on dirt or gravel roads. I included them not only because of their numbers, close proximity to one another, and ease of accessibility, but also because they are set in the midst of mountains and some of the oldest forest in the province. You reach them by travelling through a beautiful valley with views of waterfalls, high rock screes, snowcapped mountains, dense forests, turbulent rivers, and countless streams. The paved road follows the ever-changing Chilliwack River and terminates at enormous, 1198-hectare Chilliwack Lake (at an elevation of 620 metres), adding picture-postcard splendour to the journey. There is a wealth of opportunities for the angler, hiker, boater, and outdoors enthusiast.

History

The area has been settled for hundreds of years, initially by the Halq'emeylem people, who recognised the fishing and hunting potential. The word *Chilliwack* is taken from the Halq'emeylem language and means "backwater travelling." The region is adjacent to the United States and a monument in Sapper Park, at the far end of Chilliwack Lake, commemorates the British Royal Engineers who mapped the border. The area has been intensively logged and this industry continues in the area today, as you can see by the maze of logging roads that scar the landscape and the evidence of logging on the mountains.

Location and facilities

All the campgrounds are located southwest of Chilliwack. To find them, follow the signs for Chilliwack Lake Provincial Park from Highway 1, taking a well-signposted turnoff at Vedder Crossing (four kilometres south of Highway 1) onto Chilliwack Lake Road. The road is paved for the first 34 kilometres, after which it becomes a good gravel road. This scenic, quiet road leads to the sites. All services can be found in Chilliwack, while the Pointa Vista Store, 10 kilometres from Vedder Crossing, has basic provisions and a cafe. I list the campgrounds from west to east.

Tamihi Creek

You will find the first campground just as Chilliwack Lake Road crosses the Chilliwack River (10 kilometres from Vedder Crossing). With the exception of the toilets, it is almost as good as a provincial park. Upon crossing the river, turn right onto the Tamihi Forest Service Road and drive .5 kilometres to the site. The campground has space for about 30 parties, who can choose between a large, grassy, camping area with a few poplar trees, picnic tables, and toilets (the more desirable spots), or heavily wooded sites that are a little overgrown. This is one of only two BCFS

locations along Chilliwack Lake Road that can easily accommodate the larger recreational vehicle (the other being Thurston Meadows). The sound of rushing water is ever present at this campground, which is close to the rapids where Tamihi Creek and the Chilliwack River meet.

Tamihi Creek can accommodate larger recreational vehicles.

Allison Pool

Thirteen and a half kilometres from Vedder Crossing is a gravel access road that leads to the second BCFS campsite, renowned among the fishing fraternity as one of the best spots for steelhead in the region. Although you can drive right up to a couple of the camping spots, most require a walk-in of 500 metres or so, which is well worth the effort when you find a spot on the sand by the water's edge. There are about 15 spaces in total.

Thurston Meadows

This riverside campground is set in an open, grassy area—an unusual feature for a BCFS site. Drive 17 kilometres from Vedder Crossing, then take a gravel road to the left. Several camping spots are set on a circle road that is easy driving even in the largest RV. Some of the 15 sites are on the water's edge and some are set amidst the privacy of trees. There are concrete picnic tables at every spot as well as fire pits, and it is possible to launch canoes and kayaks from the day-use area. It's great to watch the white-water enthusiasts travel by.

Pierce Creek

This spot serves more as a parking lot for those who want to climb the Pierce Lake Trail, but there is space for a maximum of five camping parties.

To reach the site, turn off Chilliwack Lake Road 22 kilometres from Vedder Crossing. The half-kilometre access road runs between two sections of correctional institution land. There is a toilet and one picnic table but little else, making this the least desirable location of them all.

Riverside

There is accommodation here for about 10 parties. It is 30 kilometres from Vedder Crossing, just as Chilliwack Lake Road crosses the river. The campsites are strung out along the gravel access road and are quite open. Like many of the other sites, it is hemmed in by the forested mountains that dominate the valley. The sound of running water and the massive Douglas firs make this a relaxing, therapeutic venue in which to pitch a tent.

Post Creek

This is one of the most popular BCFS sites along the road, and it frequently takes overspill from Chilliwack Lake Provincial Park. Thirty-nine kilometres from Vedder Crossing, watch for a gravel access road with a sign marking the Centennial Trail. There are camping areas on both sides of the creek with accommodation for about 20 parties. The east side of the creek has the better spots, but during the weekends it is used as a car park by hikers exploring the trails that lead from the site, so it can appear crowded. There are picnic tables, fire rings, and toilets here. The west side, accessed via a gravel road 38 kilometres from Vedder Crossing, tends to be quieter but is further from the water. Post Creek is best avoided at weekends but is fantastic if you find it when no one else is there.

Paleface Creek

This may be the best free camping spot along the route, but many have recognised its merits so it can be crowded. Located 46.5 kilometres from Vedder Crossing (you'll be driving on a good gravel road for the last 12.5 kilometres), the campground is well situated and has access to a boat launch. About 15 sites are available quite close to the road (which is not busy) under large, shady fir trees with views of the lake and running waters. There are lots of picnic tables, fire pits, and toilets.

Depot Creek

This lovely site is set on a gravel arm that stretches into Chilliwack Lake and has the additional advantage of offering a beach (if the lake waters are not at their highest level). You will find it by travelling 50 kilometres from Vedder Crossing and crossing the bridge at Depot Creek. There are about 15 camping spaces set in an area of thick forest that makes them appear very dark. The access road is somewhat tortuous.

Watch for kayakers on the Chilliwack River.
This is home to Canada's Olympic kayak team.

Recreational activities

Hiking

There are a variety of hiking trails in the region. The most popular campsite if you aim to hike is Post Creek, as there are a number of trails leading directly from this spot. They include the Flora Lake Trail, the Greendrop Trail, and the Radium Lake Trail. The Centennial Trail also runs through the area. At the Riverside site, hikers can easily access the Ford Mountain Trail and the Williams Ridge Trail. As mentioned above, the Pierce Lake Trail leads from the Pierce Creek BCFS site, but it is reputed to be difficult and overgrown. Before walking one of these trails you should ensure you have the proper equipment, including maps and a guidebook—refer to the ones listed in the appendix.

Boating

The best boat-launching facility is at Chilliwack Lake Provincial Park, but Paleface Creek also has a gravel boat launch. Chilliwack River has become a very popular white-water location. The area is home to the Canadian Olympic kayak team, and kayakers and canoeists travel to these waters to pit their wits against the rapids. There are numerous places from which to launch a kayak (e.g., Thurston Meadows). Cross wires have been strung near the first bridge over the Chilliwack River to further test the kayakers' skill as they battle one of the most turbulent areas of the river.

Fishing

One of the area's biggest attractions is the angling in both Chilliwack Lake and Chilliwack River. The river is characterised by an interesting mixture of rushing white waters and calm green pools, and it offers steelhead, salmon, and trout fishing. It is internationally renowned for its salmon fishing. The campgrounds nearer to Vedder Crossing (especially

Allison Pool) are recognised as superior fishing venues. During the peak season, anglers crowd the most popular spots and the area is full of those who "live to fish." Chilliwack Lake contains rainbow and cutthroat trout, Dolly Varden, and whitefish.

Family activities
Allison Pool has swimming potential, as do those campsites on Chilliwack Lake. There are also beaches at Depot Creek and in Chilliwack Lake Provincial Park if the lake is not too high.

Activities adjacent to the park
The Chilliwack River Salmonid Enhancement Facility, 22 kilometres from Vedder Crossing, releases approximately 260,000 coho, chinook, chum, steelhead, and trout into the river each year. It is open to the public. Chilliwack Lake Ecological Reserve is at the far end of the lake and protects an area of old-growth forest (see the Chiliwack Lake entry in Chapter 2).

Summary
In addition to the eight BCFS campgrounds detailed here, Chilliwack Lake Road will lead you to a number of other free campsites farther from the main paved road, but all within 40 kilometres of each other. To reach many of these will require the use of a four-wheel-drive vehicle. Some of these remote sites have become regular haunts for trail bikers, so they can be noisier than you might expect. Unlike other free campgrounds, the ones detailed above are close to services and easily accessible with a vehicle, but it is not only for these practical reasons that I sing their praises. Their real advantage is the scenery and the many recreational opportunities on their doorstep.

28. Chehalis Lake/Chehalis River, BCFS

Wedged between Mount Fletcher and Mount Orrock to the west and Mount Downing to the east (with peaks towering over 1200 metres), and fed by over 20 streams, creeks, and rivers including the raging torrents of Eagle River and Skwellepil Creek, Chehalis Lake is a majestic ribbon of water about 10 kilometres long but only 1 kilometre wide. It demonstrates the wonders BCFS sites can provide for those willing to endure a rugged drive away from the crowds and into true wilderness. There are three campgrounds on the banks of the lake and each gives you a base from which to explore the backcountry. Be prepared, however, as the road is very rough in places and is not recommended for anyone driving a new car—or a car at all. It is probably best accessed by truck. For those who want to experience the wonders of this environment from a paved road, a campground at Chehalis River grants access to both cars and recreational vehicles.

History

The area has been the scene of active logging over the last century. With roads dominated by logging trucks, locals rarely explored its pristine beauty. Recently, as Lower Mainland residents began to venture into more backcountry areas (and as logging companies became more accommodating), Chehalis Valley has been recognised as an undeveloped yet interesting and accessible area of southwestern B.C. Chehalis Lake is fed by the North Chehalis River and the Eagle River, whose turbulent waters combine to create a 90-metre-deep plunge pool at the north end of the lake. This noisy, tree- and boulder-strewn area is in contrast to the quiet, clear green waters, ideal for canoeing, in other parts of the lake. Further downstream, the southern section of the Chehalis River has long been identified as an angler's dream. More recently it has become known as one of the best BCFS sites.

Location

At an elevation of 227 metres in the Chehalis Valley, 629-hectare Chehalis Lake is located 20 kilometres north of Harrison Mills. All three BCFS sites are on the Chehalis Forest Services Road that branches off Highway 7 near the Sasquatch Inn. The initial 14.7 kilometres of the forestry road are a good gravel road. After you cross Statlu Creek Bridge, the road becomes more hazardous, following the river on the right for a while before turning and climbing. At 19.8 kilometres from Highway 7, a side road leads off to the boat launch and the southernmost camping location (at 25.8 kilometres). The second campground is further along the side road (30 kilometres from Highway 7). Skwellepil Creek flows nearby and gives this second BCFS site its name. Part of this campground is high above the lake, which means there are lovely views. An access road leads steeply down to the lakeshore. Park at the top and walk down unless you have four-wheel drive. The third and most northerly campground is located a little further along Chehalis Forest Services Road (33.4 kilometres from Highway 7) and is easier for those without trucks to access. It is the largest of the three locations.

In contrast, the campground at Chehalis River is six kilometres from the same turnoff at Highway 7, but it is on the paved Mor-

The Chehalis River is wedged between canyon walls, offering you spectacular scenery.

ris Valley Road. The campground is near the bridge over the river and does not require any rough road travel. Services can be obtained on Highway 7.

Facilities

The first campground at Chehalis Lake is on the water's edge at the southern end of the lake. The campground is divided into two areas. The one near the boat launch is more suitable for large vehicles. Steps lead down to the beach from here and it is a pleasant spot if the waters of the lake are not high. The second area is less popular and quieter, being away from the boat launch. There are about ten camping spots here, set in dense vegetation. Some have picnic tables. The site has garbage cans and two toilets.

The second campground, at Skwellepil Creek, is probably the nicest but is also the most difficult to access if you are not driving a truck. These camping spots are relatively open, giving outdoor enthusiasts an uninterrupted view of the surrounding mountains—and it is only a matter of walking a few metres to sit on a rocky beach by the clear waters of the lake. Additional camping spots away from the beach offer more shade and privacy. There are about 20 sites in all to choose from. Fire rings, toilets, garbage bins, and picnic tables are all here.

The third campground must be one of the largest in the BCFS roster with about 40 sites. Some of these overlook the Eagle River while others

One of the campsites for you to enjoy.

are close to a gravel beach and Chehalis Lake. There are toilets, picnic tables, fire pits, and garbage bins.

There are three camping areas at Chehalis River, on both sides of the river. They accommodate about 40 camping parties, making it another large BCFS campground. Some sites overlook the rapids while others are in areas of heavy forest and consequently have little light. At least six toilets service the area and there are numerous concrete picnic tables and garbage cans. Recreational vehicles are easily accommodated.

Recreational activities

Hiking

The area has an impressive array of old logging roads, backroads, and tracks to explore. Anyone contemplating a serious hiking excursion into what must be regarded as wilderness should be well prepared and armed with a good map. Those who go fully equipped will not be disappointed. One note of warning: Do not attempt the Chehalis River Canyon Trail from the Chehalis River campground if you suffer from vertigo. It is a steep climb up the canyon walls that yields breathtaking views of the clear green pools below.

Boating

Chehalis Lake offers excellent boating opportunities. The main concrete boat launch is at the south end of the lake, although it is possible to launch smaller craft from the other two camping locations. You will need skill to manoeuvre to the main boat launch, as it is a little tight. There are sand spits, coves, beaches, rivers, and creeks to explore, so in this respect the lake is perfect for canoeing. The geography of the area fosters strong winds, although the southerly end of the lake is more sheltered. Chehalis

*What's he searching for
on the banks of the Chehalis River?*

River north of the campground has white-water canoeing/kayaking potential.

Fishing

The main recreational pursuit in the area is undoubtedly fishing, and the lake provides the perfect habitat for Dolly Varden (anglers tell of five-kilogram Dollys pulled from the waters), rainbow trout, and whitefish. It is possible to troll and fly-fish at the southern end of the lake. The gravel bar at Skwellepil Creek is another good fishing spot. The lake is very deep, reaching depths of 150 metres at its centre, which makes it a good place to fish from a boat. Anglers are also eager to try the waters of the numerous rivers and streams that flow into and out of the lake at different spots along the shoreline.

Chehalis River is famous for steelhead. Anglers trying their skills in the river initially developed the Chehalis River Canyon Trail.

Family activities

On the lake, the best swimming (and sunbathing) to be had is at Skwellepil Creek, where the boulders in the creek create a varied swimming haven of green pools and rapid waters. Depending on the height of the river, there may be beaches and sunbathing opportunities at the other locations.

Summary

With over 60 camping spots to choose from, the three BCFS campgrounds on Chehalis Lake offer a wilderness camping experience amongst some of the most rugged scenery in southwestern B.C. for those who can endure the rough road to the destination. The dusty, dry, potholed state of the access roads means those with a brand new RV or a car with low suspension should probably forsake the wilderness drive and pristine waters and head for the nearby alternative, Chehalis River. It is tame in comparison to Chehalis Lake, but it does have excellent camping suitable for every type of recreational vehicle. Chehalis Lake and other BCFS campgrounds located in similar remote areas justify the purchase of a truck or 4x4, but options like Chehalis River prove camping for free is not just the domain of the 4x4 owner.

29. Inland Lake, BCFS

The camping provisions at Inland Lake, sometimes called Loon Lake, make this not only one of the best free camping spots, but also one of the premier camping locations for disabled campers. While many of the larger provincial parks in the province offer facilities for wheelchairs, Inland Lake not only has ramps and larger toilets, but it also provides 13 kilometres of flat, accessible trail, six piers stretching into the lake for easy fishing from a wheelchair, slopes into the water for swimmers, and a number of camping cabins specifically designed for the physically challenged. These facilities reflect the caring nature of the surrounding community and its commitment to ensure that everyone has access to the second-growth rain forest. Inland Lake is not a secluded BCFS site; it is popular with both locals and tourists and for good reason. It is one of the best-kept BCFS sites in the province.

History

The community of Powell River grew up around the logging industry, which still dominates today. The town is named after Dr Israel Powell, at one time superintendent of Indian Affairs for British Columbia, who was active in the campaign to bring British Columbia into Confederation in 1871. At the turn of the century, Powell River was the first pulp-and-paper-based community in western Canada. There are many buildings dating back to

*Inland Lake campsite offers a number of camping cabins
specifically designed for the physically challenged.*

1910 still standing in the original townsite, including the Rodmay Hotel, Bank of Montreal, provincial courthouse, and many small houses. In 1995 the area was declared a National Historic District by the federal government.

Location

Inland Lake is situated below the 1065-metre peak of Mount Mahony and is 12 kilometres north of Powell River. To reach Powell River from the Lower Mainland, take the ferry from Horseshoe Bay to Langdale (45 minutes), drive 90 minutes to a second ferry from Earl's Cove to Saltery Bay (50 minutes), which leaves you with a 30-minute drive to the town. From Vancouver Island, take the ferry from Comox to Powell River. Turn right off Highway 101 onto Alberni Street. Go up the hill to Manson Avenue, turn left, and follow Manson to Cassiar Street. Turn right onto Cassiar (which turns into Yukon Street) and continue on to Haslam Street. Turn right on Haslam and stay on it until the first junction, where you take the left road to the campsite. It's easier than it sounds.

Facilities

As mentioned above, on the occasions I visited this campground I found it to be the best maintained of all BCFS sites. It is managed by Powell River Forestry Service, with a caretaker on site from April until October. The main campground accommodates about 15 parties, with space for large RVs, and is adjacent to the day-parking area. Pit toilets, wood (kept dry under canopies), fire pits, garbage bins, and picnic tables are in a lightly wooded area. There are pumps you can use to collect lake water, which should be boiled before use. There are four overnight camping spots at different places around the lake. They also have wood, pump water, and fire pits. Two cabins for the disabled are located at the main site and there are three at other sites around the lake. The view across the lake from these cabins is magical. Services are found in the communities of Cranberry and Powell River.

Recreational activities

Hiking

The biggest draw at Inland Lake must be the 13-kilometre flat route that circles the lake, convenient for wheelchairs or those with strollers. Kilometre markers are placed around the lake so walkers know how far they have to go. (Remember to take water.) Dotted along this trail are a series of wooden carvings of frogs, eagles, area pioneers, and others. The most impressive of these is a totem pole created by Sliammon carver Jackie Timothy. From this well-maintained gravel trail, which is entirely wheelchair accessible, you can take two footpaths: one to Lost Lake and

Send me for water anytime with a view like this!

on to Haywire Bay on Powell Lake; the other directly to Powell Lake. If you do not want to walk all around the lake, you can also hike to Anthony Island. A wooden bridge leads to the island with its picnic and camping facilities. Numerous other hiking trails exist in the region, details of which can be obtained from the Visitors Centre in Powell River.

Boating
Inland Lake is great for canoeing and kayaking. Although powerboats are permitted, they are limited to 10 horsepower engines. From Inland Lake it is possible to portage to Powell Lake (0.7 kilometres).

Cycling
Cycling is permitted on the trail.

Fishing
The 349-hectare lake contains cutthroat in moderate numbers, measuring 25 to 35 centimetres and larger, and kokanee. Seven piers are positioned around the lake to facilitate fishing. No fishing is permitted from November 1 until March 31.

Wildlife observation
In addition to the loons that give the lake its second name, eagles, ducks, ravens, crows, grouse, bluejays, and hummingbirds can also be spotted. Beavers and otters have been seen here, as have bears. Families wandering around the lake on foot often see snakes, frogs, and slugs.

Family activities
The waters of the lake are calm, clear, and warm—ideal for swimming. A small beach by the day-parking area offers sunbathing opportunities, as

do the other rocks and beaches around the lake. There are picnic tables near the day-use area overlooking the lake.

Activities adjacent to the park

Visit the Powell River Visitors Centre on Wharf Street for advice and information on the numerous activities available in town. You can visit the museum or sports complex, take a tour of the MacMillian Bloedel mill or a walking excursion around the old township, or enjoy a meal or snack in one of the coffee bars, cafes, and restaurants. Powell River promotes itself as the Dive Capital of Canada, emphasizing its clear waters and unusual sealife (see the Saltery Bay entry in Chapter 6). The community of Lund, north of town, is a pleasant place to visit, and from Lund you can take a water taxi to Savary Island, six kilometres away, with beaches comparable to those of Hawaii and warm waters for swimming. At time of writing, the return trip cost $12.00. If the weather is good it is well worth this expense. Texada Island is 35 minutes by ferry from Powell River and has a colourful history extending back into the last century, in addition to hiking and camping opportunities.

Summary

This is the best free campground in southwestern B.C. It is also the best campground for the disabled. The community of Powell River seems particularly sensitive to people with disabilities and many facilities in the town reflect this concern.

The campground and the lake are wonderful. During our last visit, the day started with grey raining skies and we set off on our hike in waterproof gear. Halfway around the trail the skies became bluer, and by the time we returned to the car we were hot and sweaty. Three families were noisily playing in the lake, proving to us it was not cold, so we got changed (in the car—no change house here yet, but I would be surprised if one is not built in a few years) and revelled in the warm water. We were there during the Labour Day weekend, when there was plenty of camping space and few people on the trail.

Staff at the Powell River Visitors Centre told us the area is a fertile breeding ground for mosquitoes—if you are planning a trip in mosquito season, be prepared. There is a donation box at this, my favourite free campground in B.C., for those who have enjoyed the facilities and want to maintain them. I hope many contribute.

30. Weaver Lake, BCFS

The appeal of this camping area is the variety of pursuits it offers the outdoor enthusiast, coupled with its beautiful setting in the Hemlock Valley. These aspects, as well as the campground's proximity to Vancouver, mean it is becoming one of the most popular free camping locations in the province.

I first discovered Weaver Lake when I had been living in B.C. for only a few months. Anxious to explore my new environment, I purchased the book *109 Walks in British Columbia's Lower Mainland* and read about a delightful trail around Weaver Lake. I set out to visit it in my 1974 Ford Pinto. What the book failed to tell was that to reach this lake in late October you had to navigate numerous potholes, cavities, and a near-river running down the trenches at the roadside before the hiking boots were donned. These hazards, as well as most of the elevation gain, were completed during the final entertaining kilometre of road, adding to the overall adventure. The moral of this story is: this campground can be reached by car, but other vehicles may give you a less stressful ride.

History

The region is home to the mythical Sasquatch, half man and half beast and said to roam about the area. As with other BCFS sites, active logging took place at the location in the past and as you walk near the lake, the evidence of logging is everywhere. The area is also well known for the excellent fishing opportunities it affords.

Location

The 81 tranquil hectares of Weaver Lake are nestled in a lushly forested environment, surrounded by the gentle mountains of the Hemlock Valley. It is easy to see why it is attractive to so many campers. In addition (and in contrast to many other BCFS camping spots), it is relatively easy to access, being only 15 kilometres from a major highway. To reach it, turn north off Highway 7 onto Morris Valley Road at the Sasquatch Inn in Harrison Mills. Eleven kilometres from the highway, just past the Weaver Creek Fish Hatchery, take the Harrison West Forest Service Road. This leads to Weaver Forest Service Road. The lake is a further 2.4 kilometres along this road—the most arduous part of the journey.

Facilities

The campground is located at the southern end of the lake near Weaver Creek. There are two camping sites and a day-use area. Depending on when you visit, the place can be deserted—in which case parking is not a problem—or extremely popular, when you may need to do some creative vehicle manoeuvring. The main camping locations are found across Weaver Creek. Most have picnic tables and fire pits and there are three toilets.

There are other camping sites before you cross the creek, some with views of the placid lake. In total there are about 15 camping spaces at this location. It is also possible to escape the crowds and camp in other areas around the lake. A well-maintained trail provides easy access to beaches and solitude. Remember to pack out what you pack in.

Recreational activities

Hiking
Denhams Trail (6.4 kilometres) leads around the lake, offering different vistas of the lake and of the many islands that rise out of the waters. The walk has a couple of lookouts where you can take photographs, and with no elevation gain it is relatively easy. There are areas along the trail where you can swim or picnic.

Boating
The lake has a small gravel boat launch. Getting your boat trailer up the final section of road will prove more of a challenge than reversing the trailer into the launch. The lake is a haven for canoeists and kayakers as it features a number of islands, an interesting shoreline, and many bays and coves to explore. The waters are also relatively calm, as the surrounding mountains protect them from winds. Watch out for deadheads.

Fishing
As with many BCFS sites, one of the biggest attractions here is the fishing. The lake is annually stocked with rainbow trout that can measure up to 50 centimetres, although catches of between 30 and 40 centimetres are more common. The best fishing is to be had from a boat, as the shoreline at the southern end of the lake is not easily accessible.

Activities adjacent to the park
Kilby General Store Museum is a two-hectare historical site in the community of Harrison Mills. The two-storey general store was built in 1904 and operated by the same family until 1976. This museum contains a working farm (with pigs, goats, and hens—a delight for children) and orchard in addition to a number of buildings that have been faithfully restored. Guides dressed in period costume provide fascinating details of the development of the area at the turn of the century. Kilby General Store Museum also boasts a gift shop and tea shop serving traditional tea and scones. Children and adults will find the museum a wonderful place to pass a number of hours reading and learning about the Fraser and Harrison Rivers' colourful past. Don't miss the photographs of huge sturgeon caught in the Fraser River.

Kilby General Store Museum, near Weaver Lake, boasts a gift shop and tea shop serving traditional tea and scones.

Summary

In addition to fishing, boating, or walking around the lake, you can spend time relaxing and reading. Although this is one of the best-known free campgrounds in B.C., it is still possible to find yourself the only visitor. For those who demand a few creature comforts, the Sasquatch Inn has a pub and restaurant and is only 15 minutes away—something to bear in mind if the heavens open.

Additional Recommendations

For those with a 4x4 and a desire to "go where no one has gone before," BCFS recreational sites provide many options. For those with other modes of transportation, there are still hundreds of accessible BCFS sites. One of the biggest challenges for those who want to camp free is finding these facilities, as few are signposted. The following publications can assist.

1. Books and maps produced by the Ministry of Forests that detail the location of recreational sites can be obtained free of charge by calling the Vancouver Forest Region Office at (250) 751-7001. (This office also covers Vancouver Island.)

2. Rychkun, Ed. (1996). *Wilderness Camping in the Lower Mainland.* Langley BC: Rychkun Recreation Publications.

3. Copeland, Kathy and Craig. (1997). *Camp Free in B.C.* Vancouver: Voice in the Wilderness Press.

APPENDIX
Useful Addresses and Literature

The following pages contain suggestions for further information that will increase your appreciation of southwestern BC. There are addresses of tourism associations and BC Parks administrative offices in addition to books and pamphlets that can help you plan a successful camping adventure.

Tourism Associations

If you are considering a vacation in this part of the country, you should contact the regional tourism associations and ask for information on the areas you plan to visit and the recreational pursuits that are of specific interest. Information is provided free of charge from:

Tourism BC
PO Box 9830, Stn. Provincial Government
Victoria, BC V8W 9W5

Tourism Association of Vancouver Island
#302, 45 Bastion Square
Victoria, BC V8W 1J1
Telephone: (250) 382-3551
Fax: (250) 382-3523

Tourism Association of Vancouver, Coast and Mountains
#204, 1755 West Broadway
Vancouver, BC V6J 4S5
Telephone: (604) 739-9011
Toll free: 1-800-667-3306
Fax: (604) 739-0153

BC Parks Information Leaflets

BC Parks produces leaflets on most of the larger provincial parks with campgrounds. These usually contain a map of the campsite and tell you where wood, toilets, water, etc., can be found. For the larger parks such as Strathcona, Golden Ears, and Manning, details of the hiking trails are also given. Because these leaflets are available, I have not included maps in this book. I strongly urge you to write and request information on the park or parks you plan to visit.

In addition to the leaflets, BC Parks produces a number of other publications to add to your enjoyment of BC parks. These include: "Mountain Flowers of BC Provincial Parks," "Principal Trees of Provincial Parks," "Campground Critters of Provincial Parks," "Bears in Provincial Parks," "Principal Berries of Provincial Parks," and "Things to do Outdoors in BC Provincial Parks" (including a fascinating section on getting to know your ants). These information leaflets, together with information on specific campgrounds, can be collected from the visitors centres of larger parks or by writing directly to the regional director of the area of interest to you.

Vancouver District

Regional Director, BC Parks
1610 Mount Seymour Road
North Vancouver, BC V7G 1L3
Telephone (604) 929-1291
Fax: (604) 929-2425

Fraser Valley District

Regional Director, BC Parks
Cultus Lake Park
PO Box 3010
Cultus Lake, BC V2R 5H6
Telephone: (604) 824-2300
Fax: (604) 858-4905

Garibaldi/Sunshine District

Regional Director, BC Parks
Alice Lake Park
Box 220
Brackendale, BC V0N 1H0
Telephone: (604) 898-3678
Fax: (604) 898-4171

Strathcona District

Regional Director, BC Parks
Rathtrevor Beach Park
Box 1479
Parksville, BC V9P 2H4
Telephone: (250) 954-4600
Fax: (250) 248-8584

South Vancouver Island District

Regional Director, BC Parks
RR#6
2930 Trans-Canada Highway
Victoria, BC V9B 5T9
Telephone: (250) 391-2300
Fax: (250) 478-9211

BC Parks Headquarters

The Information Officer,
BC Parks
Second Floor, 800 Johnson Street
Victoria, BC V8V 1X4
Telephone: (250) 387-5002
Fax: (250) 387-5757

BC Parks information is also available on the Internet at
http://www.env.gov.bc.ca

For information on Pacific Rim National Park contact:

Pacific Rim National Park
Box 280
Ucuelet, BC V0R 3A0
Telephone: (250) 726-4212
(250) 726-7721

Information on Forestry Service recreational sites in southwestern B.C.
is available by writing to:

The Vancouver Forest Region Office
2100 Labieux Road
Nanaimo, BC V9T 6E9
Telephone: (250) 751-7001
Fax: (250) 751-7190

BC Ferries
Information and schedules for BC Ferries are available in Vancouver by
calling (604) 277-0277, in Victoria at (250) 381-5335, and elsewhere by
dialling 1-888-223-3779, by writing to B.C. Ferries, 1112 Fort St., Victoria,
BC, V8V 4V2, or by visiting their web site at http://www.bcferries.bc.ca.

Helpful Books and Guides

General Camping Guides
Logue, Victoria. (1995). *Camping in the 90s: Tips, Techniques and Secrets.*
    Birmingham, AL: Menasha Ridge Press.
Schneider, Bill. (1996). *Bear Aware: Hiking and Camping in Bear Country.* Falcon
    Press Publishing Co.
Seagrave, Jayne. (1998). *Provincial and National Park Campgrounds in British
    Columbia: A Complete Guide.* Second edition. Surrey, BC: Heritage House.

Camping with Children Guides
Boga, Steve. (1995). *Camping and Backpacking with Children.* Mechanicsburg,
    PA: Stackpole Books.
Cary, Alice. (1997). *Parents' Guide to Hiking and Camping.* New York: W.W.
    Norton.
Woodson, R. Dodge. (1995). *The Parent's Guide to Camping with Children.*
    Cincinnati, OH: Betterway Books.

Hiking/Walking Guides

Christie, Jack. (1996). *Whistler Outdoors Guide*. Vancouver: Douglas and McIntyre.

Copeland, Kathy and Craig. (1996). *Don't Waste Your Time in the Canadian Coast Mountains*. Vancouver: Voice in the Wilderness Press.

Kahn, Charles. (1995). *Hiking the Gulf Islands*. Victoria: Orca Book Publishers.

Macaree, Mary and David. (1994). *109 Walks in British Columbia's Lower Mainland*. Vancouver: Douglas and McIntyre.

Macaree, Mary and David. (1994). *103 Hikes in Southwestern British Columbia*. Vancouver: Douglas and McIntyre.

Obee, Bruce. (1995). *The Pacific Rim Explorer*. Vancouver: Whitecap Books.

Rutter, Jim. (1992). *Hiking Trails III: Central and Northern Vancouver Island and Quadra Island*. Victoria: Vancouver Island Trails Information Society

Stoltmann, Randy. (1996). *Hiking the Ancient Forests of BC and Washington*. Vancouver: Lone Pine Publishing.

Stone, Randy. (1996). *Hiking Guide to the Vancouver Island Backbone*. Heriot Bay, BC: Alpine Pacific Images.

Gulf Island Guides

Obee, Bruce. (1995). *The Gulf Islands Explorer*. Vancouver: Whitecap Books.

Marine Park Guides

Chettleburgh, Peter. (1985). *An Explorer's Guide to the Marine Parks of BC*. Vancouver: Special Interest Publications.

Wolferstan, Bill. (1991). *Cruising Guide to BC Volume I: Gulf Islands and Vancouver Island from Sooke to Courtenay*. Vancouver: Whitecap Books.

Wolferstan, Bill. (1991). *Cruising Guide to BC Volume II: Desolation Sound and the Discovery Islands*. Vancouver: Whitecap Books.

Free Camping Guides

Copeland, Kathy and Craig. (1997). *Camp Free in B.C.* Vancouver: Voice in the Wilderness Press.

Rychkun, Ed. (1996). *Wilderness Camping in the Lower Mainland*. Langley BC: Rychkun Recreation Publications.

Maps

British Columbia Recreational Atlas. Victoria: Province of BC—Ministry of Environment, Lands and Parks.

HERITAGE BOOKS
to help you enjoy your outdoor activities

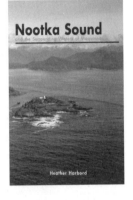

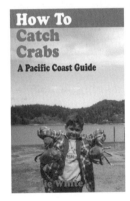

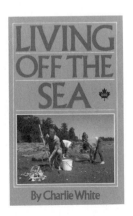

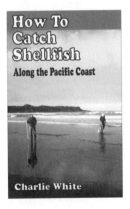

More popular books to help you enjoy your camping experience.

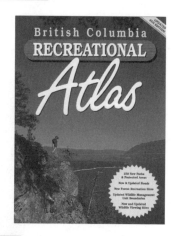

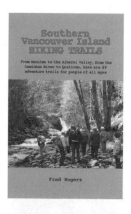

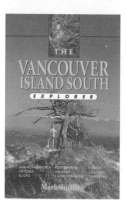

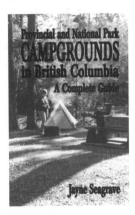

Jayne's first book, *Provincial and National Park Campgrounds in British Columbia, A Complete Guide,* sold out in one month. This second edition has been updated and is now complete with maps and campground recipes.

Over 25,000,000 visitors enjoy provincial park visits every year. With the support of BC Parks, Jayne Seagrave brings us an up-to-date documentation of all provincial and national campground facilities in BC and provides an insightful commentary based on her personal visits to individual parks.

Complete with photos and regional breakdowns, all facilities and amenities are reviewed.

BC's five most popular leisure activities are beach time, day hiking, swimming, camping, and fishing. Jayne makes these the focus of her commentary on all parks. Also included are Jayne's recommended stops for 7-, 14-, and 21-day touring excursions in different parts of the province.

This book has rapidly become the best-selling camping book in BC.

Pick up your copy of the second edition now as the 1998 print run will be limited.

ISBN 1-895811-53-8   5 1/2" x 8 1/2" • 224 pages
Softcover • $17.95

Author Jayne Seagrave camping on Newcastle Island.

Jayne Seagrave lives in East Vancouver with her husband, Andrew Dewberry. She holds a Ph.D. in Criminology and divides her time between academic research, working as the marketing manager for The Vancouver Tool Corp, and camping, travelling, and exploring the province of British Columbia.